Assessment Strategies for Elementary Physical Education

Assessment Strategies for Elementary Physical Education

Suzann Schiemer

Human Kinetics

Library of Congress Cataloging-in-Publication Data

Schiemer, Suzann, 1956-
      Assessment strategies for elementary physical education
   / Suzann Schiemer.
         p.   cm.
   Includes bibliographical references (p.)
   ISBN 0-88011-569-6
   1. Physical fitness--Testing.   2. Physical education and training-
   -Study and teaching (Elementary)   I. Title.
   GV436.S27   1999
   372.86--dc21   99-20580
                                                                            CIP

ISBN: 0-88011-569-6

Acquisitions Editor: Scott Wikgren; **Developmental Editor:** C.E. Petit, JD; **Assistant Editors:** Phil Natividad and John Wentworth; **Copyeditor:** Bonnie Pettifor; **Proofreader:** Kathy Bennett; **Graphic Designer:** Nancy Rasmus; **Graphic Artist:** Kathleen Boudreau-Fuoss; **Photo Editor:** Tom Roberts; **Cover Designer:** Jack W. Davis; **Photographer (cover):** Tom Roberts; **Illustrator:** Susan Carson; **Printer:** Versa Press

Human Kinetics books are available at special discounts for bulk purchase. Special editions or book excerpts can also be created to specification. For details, contact the Special Sales Manager at Human Kinetics.

Printed in the United States of America   10 9 8 7 6 5 4 3 2 1

Human Kinetics
Web site: http://www.humankinetics.com/

United States: Human Kinetics, P.O. Box 5076, Champaign, IL 61825-5076
1-800-747-4457
e-mail: humank@hkusa.com

Canada: Human Kinetics, 475 Devonshire Road Unit 100, Windsor, ON N8Y 2L5
1-800-465-7301 (in Canada only)
e-mail: humank@hkcanada.com

Europe: Human Kinetics, P.O. Box IW14, Leeds LS16 6TR, United Kingdom
+44 (0)113-278 1708
e-mail: humank@hkeurope.com

Australia: Human Kinetics, 57A Price Avenue, Lower Mitcham, South Australia 5062
(088) 277 1555
e-mail: humank@hkaustralia.com

New Zealand: Human Kinetics, P.O. Box 105-231, Auckland Central
(09) 523 3462
e-mail: humank@hknewz.com

Contents

Preface

"Evaluation Without Insanity" was the title of my first presentation dealing with assessment. I remember the importance of coming up with a catchy title in order to attract *anyone* to an assessment presentation. The only goal of the presentation was to generate some excitement among my peers for assessing student learning.

Assessing student learning has received considerable attention in the school reform movement. Many articles, journal features, books, conferences, and workshops in a variety of disciplines have provided educators with volumes of assessment information. Among the various disciplines, common assessment themes have emerged. Educators are using these themes as a theoretical basis for improving student assessment. The following four themes have far-reaching assessment implications in a variety of educational settings.

1. Assessment drives instruction. No longer is student assessment viewed as a final or end product. Instead, frequent assessment (formative evaluation) of the student's skills, knowledge, and behaviors is expected. Educators use the information gathered from these formative evaluations to design student-centered lessons and units.

2. Teachers should assess the critical content across the psychomotor, cogni-

tive, and affective domains (skills, knowledge, and behaviors). Today, we are living in an era of information overload. In the time allotted during the school day, it is impossible to teach and assess every bit of information. Selecting critical course content requires the educator to make very difficult choices. Even more difficult is the task of designing assessment strategies that truly measure student competence in using critical content.

3. Teachers should assess beyond the knowledge level. The real world requires students to apply information and perform competently. Students need to participate in assessment strategies designed to demonstrate abilities in the areas of comprehension, interpretation, application, analysis, synthesis, and evaluation.

4. Teachers must use a balanced approach when selecting assessment strategies. Educators need to look beyond the standardized tests for measuring student learning. As we'll see in chapters 1 through 4, you should use a variety of assessment tools reflecting traditional, alternative, and authentic assessment principals. Include a balance of assessment strategies that measure competence in process skills and end product results.

Today, I no longer need a catchy title to attract participants to an assessment workshop. The educational reform movement provided educators from all disciplines with an opportunity to revisit the hows and whys of assessing student learning. In the field of physical education, the "Definition of a Physically Educated Person" document first outlined in *Physical Education Outcomes* (Franck, et al. 1991) and the information found in *Moving Into the Future: National Standards for Physical Education* (NASPE 1995) have highlighted the crucial role assessment serves in developing the physically educated person.

The goal of this book is to help the elementary physical education specialist in designing and implementing assessment strategies. In order to meet this goal I have focused on three areas critical for successfully assessing student learning.

1. Bridge the gap between theory and practice in assessment.

2. Develop assessment tools that reflect the four E's:

   Educational—Quality assessments are designed to reflect the content and concepts of the information intentionally taught and reinforced in the lesson or lessons.

   Efficient—Quality assessments are designed to quickly collect information on student learning.

   Effective—Quality assessments are designed to accurately measure what the student has learned in the lesson or lessons.

   Enjoyable—Quality assessments allow students to share their growth and development in a variety of ways. Students are encouraged to express their understanding in a way that is meaningful in their lives. When students are permitted to share through their experiences and perceptions, teachers are able to gather a more personal view of the students they are teaching.

3. Answer the questions or concerns practitioners have regarding assessing student learning.

In part I of this book, I answer assessment questions that teachers have asked me in the past several years at assessment workshops and presentations. In doing so, I have focused on helping you deal with real life: All the theory is embedded in practical applications.

In part II, I show you how to apply the theory to individual assessment worksheets. The worksheets and strategies in this part focus on assessing the skills and concepts presented during one class period or lesson. You can use these ready-made assessment worksheets as is or tailor them to your needs. With each worksheet, you will find teaching tips to use and extensions you may wish to use in your program and then assess. These reflect the areas of motor development (critical elements of a skill), critical thinking (application of skills and concepts in a variety of settings), and language development (communication skills through the use of descriptive and expressive language).

In part III, I provide a variety of assessment strategies you can use as multiple lesson or unit-level assessments. Sample assessments in this part require students to progress through Bloom's Taxonomy to the synthesis level (the progression is knowledge, comprehension, application, analysis, synthesis, evaluation). At this level, students demonstrate their competence in planning, reorganizing, and reconstructing information.

Quality assessments should measure the student's level of mastery. As the physical educator moves from using traditional assessment strategies to alternative and authentic assessment strategies, he or she will need to design lessons that enable students to use skills from the upper end of the taxonomy. Alternative and authentic assessment strategies answer this need by requiring students to use the skills of application, analysis, synthesis, and evaluation.

Acknowledgments

And so the journey began, continued, and finally came to a close with tremendous support and encouragement from many individuals. I could never thank them all or thank them enough. To everyone listed and not listed: an eternal thank you!

To my family, Ron Haas, Tawny, Dusty, Manni, and Sienna; my parents Tom and LaVerne Schiemer; my administrators Dr. Alex Dubil, Karen Hess, and Shelley Crawford; professional mentors and colleagues George Graham, Jere Gallagher, Rick Swalm, Laura Borsdorf, Ginny Ward, Betsy McKinley, Marvin Stoner, and Marian Franck; good friends Sherry Moyer and Sue Shuman; staff at Human Kinetics, especially Scott Wikgren, Kris Ding, Kathleen Boudreau-Fuoss, and John Wentworth; and all my students at Beaver-Main and Memorial Schools. Thanks forever!

Chapter 1

Why Should I Assess Student Learning?

Simply stated, *assessment* is using collected data to measure student learning. During the past decade, assessing student learning has received increasing attention from administrators, educators, and parents. Each of these groups recognizes assessing student performance as a meaningful component in the teaching-learning process. Assessing student learning is challenging, however, and requires substantial preplanning in the areas of management, scoring, record-keeping, and evaluation (grading).

Types of Assessment

Assessment is *authentic* "if the student demonstrates the desired behavior in real-life situations rather than in artificial or contrived settings" (Melograno 1998). Providing students with real-life situations for assessing student learning is very challenging in any

discipline. In physical education, we need to look toward developing authentic assessments that allow each student to apply their skills and knowledge in a way that is personally meaningful both within and outside of the confines of the structured physical education program. Assessments in which students utilize the principles of goal setting to achieve a health-related fitness goal or utilize skills and knowledge to participate in a physical activity of personal choice are examples of meaningful authentic assessment.

Alternative assessments become authentic when applied in real-life situations (NASPE 1995). Alternative assessments require students to use higher-order thinking skills, such as problem-solving and decision-making skills. Students demonstrate knowledge, skills, and behaviors in a fairly controlled setting as opposed to real-life situations. In this book, several of the worksheets have examples of alternative assessments.

This is different from *traditional* assessment, which uses one-dimensional measurements based on a single setting. A major concern with traditional assessment strategies is the limited test content. Examples from the field of physical education are single motor skill tests, fitness tests (not used to guide lesson planning), and written tests of sport history or rules. Traditional assessments often take the form of true-false and multiple choice tests.

In physical education, developmentally appropriate authentic or alternative assessment results in teacher decisions based primarily on ongoing individual assessment of children as they participate in physical education class activities (formative evaluation), not only on test scores (summative evaluation) (Graham 1992). A student should progress in the psychomotor, affective, and cognitive domains, developing positive skills, attitudes, and knowledge about physical education.

Managing Assessment

When you look at the typical teaching load physical educators carry, it is not hard to see just how challenging assessing student learning can be! Physical educators are up against some unbelievable constraints: large numbers of students, insufficient actual instructional time, and lack of assessment and other educational materials. At the elementary level, physical educators are often responsible for providing instruction to the entire student body at one or even two schools. With this type of scheduling, it is not unusual for a physical educator to have over 500 student contacts per week. In addition, throughout the United States, some elementary physical educators are dealing with class sizes of 60 or more students (with or without an aide).

Not surprisingly, elementary physical education specialists find they have very little teaching time available (see table 1.1). Kelly (1989) provided a formula that calculated the number of physical education learning hours based on the number of days of instruction per week (see table 1.2). According to his calculations, practitioners who meet their students once a week for a 30-minute class have 8.1 hours of actual learning time for the entire school year—the actual time available to the student for on-task practice.

In addition, the issues of large class sizes and limited teaching time are often confounded by the lack of materials available for teaching and assessing student learning.

Table 1.1 Annual Time Available in Physical Education by Number of Days of Instruction Per Week for a 36-Week School Year

Days of Instruction per week	1	2	3	4	5
Total instructional days available per year	36	72	108	144	180
Minutes per class	30	30	30	30	30
Total time scheduled per year in minutes	1,080	2,160	3,240	4,320	5,400
Uncontrolled lost instructional time	108	216	324	432	540
Available instructional time per year in minutes	972	1,944	2,916	3,888	4,860
Available instructional time per year in hours	16.2	32.4	48.6	64.8	81.0
Actual learning time per year in hours assuming 50% on-task time	8.1	16.2	24.3	32.3	40.5

Table 1.2   Method for Calculating Amount of Available Instructional Time and the Number of Objectives That Can Be Addressed

A = # of weeks of school per year: 36

B = # of days of instruction per week: 2

C = Length of instructional period in minutes: 30

D = Instructional time available per year: A (36) $\times$ B (2) $\times$ C (30) = 2,160

E = Adjustment for lost instructional days: D (2,160) $\times$ .9 = 1,944

F = Estimated on-task time percentage: 50% (.5)

G = Actual instructional/learning time available: E (1,944) $\times$ F (.5) = 972

H = Time converted from minutes to hours: G (972)/60 = 16.2

I = # of objectives to be taught in a given year: 25

J = Average time available to teach each objective: H (16.2)/I (25) = .65 hours or 39 minutes.

From Kelly, 1989, "Instructional Time: The Overlooked Factor in PE Curriculum Development, *Journal of Physical Education, Recreation and Dance* 60(6):29-32. Used with permission.

In some school systems, for example, the physical education specialists are still justifying the need for one ball, one jump rope, one piece of equipment for each student in the class. This administrative attitude makes acquiring the additional materials for assessing student learning, such as paper, pencils, folders, videotapes, camcorders, and computers, all the more daunting.

So is assessing student learning a waste of time? A dream only attainable on paper? The answer is an emphatic "No!" Such a view would be a disservice to our students, our profession, our physical education programs, and ourselves. Indeed, assessing student learning offers many positive aspects that can only strengthen this profes-sion.

Identify Program Effectiveness— Strengths and Weaknesses

Many school districts across the United States have set plans for curriculum review and revision. This approach must extend into the realm of physical education, because assessing student learning based on the standards of the school district curriculum can provide important data as to the strengths and weaknesses of the physical education program. You can then use this information to develop a more effective physical education program.

Determine Competence

Student learning standards set the criteria for demonstrating competence in a particular skill. In turn, by designing assessments that reflect those standards, educators can determine student competence. If a student demonstrates competence during a preassess-ment, you should design appropriate instructional activities to challenge this student, rather than expecting this student to "relearn" something he already knows alongside his classmates. In contrast, other students may not be able to demonstrate competence of the educational standards in the time allotted in the curriculum. For those students, you will need to develop a plan for providing additional instructional and practice time.

Design Appropriate Instruction

Without assessment data, teachers often end up planning lessons and units based on their needs and interests rather than their students' needs. But assessment data empowers you to reflect on the learning that did or did not take place during the lesson or unit. Then you should use the assessment data when planning the next series of learning experiences to help you meet the needs of all the students in the class.

Measure Individual Progress

On occasion, you may encounter a student who, due to prior experiences such as private lessons, is extremely proficient in the

skills you are presenting in a unit. Yet, although this child enters the program at a high level of skill, she decides not to challenge herself to make any improvement during the unit, despite your efforts to provide challenges tailored to her needs. At the same time, you may have a student who has no prior experience in the skills you are presenting, but who shows tremendous growth during the unit. Still, he is far from using the skills proficiently. Here's the dilemma: Which child should receive the "A" or "O" ("outstanding") on his or her report card? How would you justify the grades you assign to the parents of the skilled child and unskilled child? Tough questions!

Assessment data provides part of the answer because you can use it to measure the individual progress of each student. With vastly varying motor ability levels, prior experience, and academic abilities of students in our physical education classes, we need to use assessment data to measure the progress of each child, instead of comparing one child to another.

Determine the Need for Remedial and Accelerated Activities

When we can identify each student's needs through assessment, we can then begin to individualize our instruction, providing the appropriate class activities for each student. Although all the students may be working on the underhand throw, for example, we can provide remedial and accelerated activities by modifying equipment and providing intratask variations (a technique in which the teacher modifies a task based on the abilities and interests of the children [Graham 1992]). Intratask variations are teacher-driven and can make the task easier or more challenging. Changing the size of the ball, shape of the ball, or the number of times the student must successfully perform the skill are examples of intratask variations.

Summary

Assessment is a critical aspect of good program and classroom management. It provides us the data we need to develop and evaluate our physical education programs. It is also the foundation for ensuring that our students learn the physical education skills that they will need later in school and in life.

Chapter 2

How Do I Manage This Thing Called *Assessment*?

Physical educators often hesitate to assess student learning. Many times, this is due to the perception that assessment takes too much time away from class instruction. This perception may be based on the teacher's own past experiences as a student and as an educator. Perhaps you remember skill testing for which the entire class stood in a line while each student performed the motor skills "X" number of times. Or, maybe your memories involve the written test, which consisted of two or three pages of questions related to a sport and took an entire class period to complete.

These past assessment models are not practical or effective for the elementary physical education program, especially one that meets one, two, or three times a week. For this reason, I have designed many of the assessment strategies in this book so that you can implement and complete them in less than one or two minutes. What's the secret? All you need are careful preplanning and a few practice opportunities for the students to learn the assessment protocols. Assessment protocols provide students with an organized method for obtaining the assessment materials (i.e., paper, pencil, or portfolio), selecting a private area in the gym to complete the assessment, and collecting the materials at the end of the assessment episode. When you initiate a plan for assessing student learning, the students will make mistakes in following your directions; this is a normal part of the learning process. Instead of feeling frustrated, turn the situation into a teachable moment and have students practice helpful assessment protocols, such as using their portfolio folders as mini-offices. If possible, involve the students in designing a solution for a problem. One year my students came up with the idea that portfolio folders are a perfect way to provide a private space for completing written assessment work. The students simply open the folder and stand it on end, creating a small study carrel that the students called "their private office."

This chapter will highlight some of the common frustrations you may have when initiating assessment strategies and solutions that have worked for me. Although my solutions will not remedy every situation, I encourage you to modify, rework, or adapt my suggestions to fit your needs.

Basic assessment protocols will be shared such as:

- using color coding as a means to facilitate the distribution and collection of assessment equipment and materials,
- utilizing student/class aides to check assessment sheets for names and dates, and
- the use of low-end technology (e.g., tape recorder) in meeting the various learning support adaptations for students.

Frustration 1: Distribution of Assessment Materials

The first assessment protocol students should learn has to do with the location of and distribution procedures for assessment materials—crucial factors in assessment management. For starters, passing out papers and pencils is time consuming! In order to streamline the process, I organize my students into color-coded learning teams (e.g., blue, green, red, and yellow). Each of the four teams has an equipment area that contains the class equipment for the lesson (e.g., balls, rackets) and the assessment materials necessary for the class (e.g., papers and pencils). This strategy works well as long as the learning teams have eight or fewer students. Learning teams consisting of more than eight students will slow down the distribution process. So for larger classes, increase the number of color-coded learning teams to keep team size small.

Before class, I place the necessary number of worksheets and record sheets in a plastic box, bin, or bucket and pencils in their own small container. When I require students to use equipment, they automatically report to their learning team equipment area, select the appropriate equipment, and return to self-space to begin working. I don't have to give these instructions after the first few classes. To make things easier, I have color-coded the equipment containers for each learning team; for example, the blue learning team has a large blue bucket to hold equipment, a blue office file holder for papers, and a blue basket for pencils. In the past, I have used crayons and colored pencils matching the learning team color for students to write with. Crayons were unpopular with the students, however, because they could not neatly change their answers when they made a mistake. Switching to colored pencils with erasers worked better for the students and provided me with an easier way to identify papers on which students forgot to put their names.

Frustration 2: Collecting Assessments

Collecting student assessment sheets by the learning team will allow you to quickly score and record the information gathered during that class period. Give one student in each learning team the job of organizing the team's papers; this is great organizational activity that helps children learn responsibility. In addition, I paper-clip each class's assessment sheets to the daily lesson plan and record sheet. That way, when I review the information at a later time, everything is together.

Frustration 3: Dating Assessments

Placing the correct date on an assessment sheet is very important if you are going to file assessments in a portfolio. Yet even in the best situations, students are not always accurate at dating their own papers. I found that by purchasing a library date stamp and stamp pads I could quickly and accurately date student papers. This is also an activity that students like to help you with. You might place a stamp and pad at each learning team's equipment station. You can use a different color of ink to indicate each marking period or different years. For example, you might have your first-graders use red ink, your second-graders always use green ink, and so on, so you can quickly see what grade a child was in when you review the worksheets in later years.

Frustration 4: Getting Names on Papers

When you are dealing with large numbers of students, it is extremely frustrating to find that one student, or two or three, has not written his or her name on the worksheet. But with a little planning and effort, you can easily correct this problem.

As soon as the students get their pencils, instruct them to put their names on the papers. Then prior to reading any of the questions aloud again, remind the students to put their names on their papers. As the students are turning in their papers, remind them one more time to add their names. As the school year progresses, you will find that you can reduce the number of times you remind the students to put their names on their papers. With some classes, you might have the class vote on a signal to use, such as clapping three times, instead of the verbal reminder about names.

The following strategies are especially effective with younger children at the beginning of the school year:

- Buddy name checks—Each student has an in-class partner responsible for name checking prior to the paper's being collected. This strategy works well with students experiencing difficulty with handwriting or language skills, as the partner can assist in getting the name on the paper.
- Team name check—Assign one person from each learning team to collect the papers and check for names.
- Name check farewell—As each student leaves the gymnasium he or she hands the paper to you. You must see the name on the paper before you will bid the student farewell.
- Teacher aides—Request that teacher aides be scheduled to assist you in physical education class (for roll taking, reading written material for nonreaders, station monitors, and so on). Such aides can serve as a valuable resource in assisting students with physical, academic, social, and communication challenges. One of the class duties of the aide could be making sure all papers have a name at the top.

As you look through the assessment worksheets in this book, you will find another strategy I use to encourage students to put their names on their papers. On the top of each worksheet, you will see the words "Full name." At the bottom of the assessment worksheet, you again see the words "Full name" in a scoring box. Any student who writes his or her first and last name on the paper receives one extra point. A first

Rose K., by Any Other Name

In the beginning of the school year, I often have students writing their first name and last initial—not very helpful when you have three Michael B's in your class! Some of your students will write their *entire* full name—first, middle, and last; personally, I have no problem with this choice. However, when the students begin to ask me how to spell their middle names I reply, "Don't worry about the spelling of your middle name—just sound it out." This is a technique used in the classroom called *inventive spelling*. If necessary, you could then work with the classroom teacher to develop strategies for learning how to spell last names.

name, last initial, or first name only receives a half point. This strategy works well in reducing the number of papers without names. Then, as the students become accustomed to placing their names on their papers, you can take the "Full name" criteria out of the scoring box.

You may also notice that the sample worksheets contain the words Blue, Green, Red, and Yellow. Since the students are divided into learning teams by color, I find it useful for them to identify their learning team on the worksheet by circling the correct color word. This strategy also helps the students remember what learning team they belong to. With young children, you may want to use the corresponding color highlighter to emphasize the color word. Parent volunteers and older students can be a big help in getting papers ready for classroom use. If you use this strategy, you can also award a point for identifying the learning team in the scoring box.

When assessing nonphysical education elements, it is important to identify and communicate to students the elements you plan to use and define the levels of competency students must demonstrate. Then include this information on the scoring rubric.

Frustration 5: Teaching Back-to-Back Classes

It is common for elementary specialists to teach back-to-back classes of varying grade levels. For example, one period with first graders, then the next period with fifth graders, then third graders, and so on. Naturally, this creates a special problem for arranging assessment materials (not to mention lesson equipment!). To answer this challenge, use folders (color-coded to match the learning team, of course) that contain the assessment worksheets and/or record sheets to be used during that class period. Label the front of each folder with the grade or homeroom. Train students to find the folder with their grade number or homeroom on it and take the worksheets or record sheets from that folder.

Frustration 6: Teaching Nonreaders and Non-English-Speaking Students

By making a tape recording of your assessment materials you are not penalizing the nonreaders in your class. You can play the tape during the assessment to help the entire class follow along. This strategy has much to offer both you and your students. The students may choose to follow along with the tape or proceed at their own pace. Meanwhile, you are free to monitor and assist the students. To help non-English-speaking students, you may wish to find an individual who can translate the assessment into the student's primary language. Other strategies for non-English-speaking students include presenting information in a pictorial form through the use of illustrations, diagrams, and videotapes. Students may also use gestures and basic sign language skills to provide assessment information.

Frustration 7: Dealing With Insufficient Assessment Materials

Often physical educators are working with very tight budgets, which barely cover the costs of their program needs let alone support the costs of assessment materials. However, there are alternative methods to obtain the assessment supplies you need.

Paper

For years I searched the supply room for old reject paper that no one else would use. It's amazing how many reams of old ditto paper, manila paper, lined handwriting paper, and construction paper a persistent teacher can find and use for assessment. I've also used white copy paper printed on one side only. By putting this paper in my computer printer, I have recycled the blank side of the paper for printing assessment materials. Or I cut the paper into quarter sheets on which students

When making a tape recording of an assessment, keep the following points in mind:
- Pause long enough in between each question to provide the children with thinking and responding time.
- Read through the assessment twice. During the second reading, you may shorten the pause time between questions.

write the answers to short oral quizzes. Younger children may need the back (previously used) side of the papers "X-ed out" to avoid confusion (an older student or other volunteer can do this for you).

Writing Utensils

Although pencils are the preferred tool, for years my students used crayons. At the end of each school year, I would ask other teachers for any leftover crayons. As mentioned earlier, when the students complained they couldn't erase crayon marks, we switched to colored pencils with erasers. Again at various times of the school year, I check with the art teacher for leftover pencils. Now I use a combination of colored and regular lead pencils.

In addition, don't forget to check with businesses in your community. You may find these sources to be gold mines of free materials. For example, one of our local merchants donated several boxes of pencils to our school.

Management is the key to smoothly implementing any assessment strategy. Establish the assessment protocols you learned about in this chapter to save you a lot of unnecessary headaches. In the next chapter, you will find that management strategies are also important in the areas of scoring assessments, record-keeping, and evaluation (grading). Once you have gained control of the management issues, you will then be ready to move your assessment plan forward.

Chapter 3

How Do I Score Student Assessments?

A critical component in assessment design is determining how you will score the assessment. Assessment worksheets designed to assess the knowledge level (recall of information) require the teacher to check student work for correct and incorrect responses. This reduces the teacher's workload by limiting reflection or decision making in scoring this type of assessment. The teacher guide for chapter 5 provides scoring information for the various knowledge level assessment strategies presented.

However, no longer can we settle for students only repeating the information they've learned through our lessons. Instead, assessment should allow students to demonstrate the ability to *use* information. The terms *alternative* and *authentic* assessment are used to describe assessment strategies that incorporate problem solving and decision making (alternative assessment) in real-world applications (authentic assessment). Alternative and authentic assessments assess student learning above the knowledge level: In short, a teacher who uses these assessment strategies expects students to use, examine, and apply skills and knowledge. But such real-life skills can be difficult to score objectively. You will need to reflect and make decisions very deliberately before and after each assessment to make accurate judgments about student learning.

Assessment Scoring Tools

Due to the numbers of student assessments you have to score, you should focus the scoring rubric on essential physical education skills, concepts, and knowledge. However, there may be situations (e.g., interdisciplinary team goals, integrated subject assessments, or district mandates) when you will need to assess nonphysical education elements such as the following:

- Technical writing skills, for example, correct spelling, correct use of punctuation and grammar
- Mathematical computations, for example, correct calculations of resting, working, and training heart rates
- Neatness

You can and should use a variety of assessment tools to gauge student learning. But you must have methods for accurately scoring students' work. The following sections describe two tools: the scoring rubric and the scoring box.

The Scoring Rubric

A *rubric* (scoring guide) provides an outline of the guidelines for scoring student performance. A well-designed rubric clearly identifies the essential performance criteria and can be used reliably by the teacher or an outside rater.

Currently, the two most frequently used styles in designing rubrics are holistic and analytical. A *holistic rubric* scores the student's performance as a whole. This type of rubric combines a variety of essential performance elements in order to determine the overall level of competency. The student's performance is then reflected in a single score. The holistic method of scoring is relatively easy to use and very effective in assessing large numbers of performances.

Analytical rubrics help the rater score performances based on specific essential elements. In this scoring system, students receive feedback on the level of performance for each essential element. Using an analytical rubric is time consuming, but it provides valuable individualized information for both the teacher and student. Both holistic and analytical rubrics use similar sets of components in their development. Each of the three components—essential dimensions (traits), rating scale, and key performance indicators—define a specific portion of the rubric.

A scoring rubric for each alternative and authentic assessment is essential. Though you must tailor this scoring tool for each skill you're assessing, follow these guidelines to streamline the process:

- Create a grid that has enough room for the items you need to list (see following guidelines). You can use graph paper or the table-making function in your computer's word processors to make grid templates. Then all you have to do is add the details for each assessment.
- Down the left-hand side of the grid, list the critical components you plan to assess. Examples may include appropriate use of critical elements, use of discipline-specific terminology (e.g., "aerobics" versus "heart and lung activities"), proper use of equipment, integration of knowledge, punctuation, correct spelling, neatness, and so on.
- Across the top of the grid, list the levels of performance. Usually, this information should match the reporting system you use on the student report card. Examples include percentages; O, S, NI (Outstanding, Satisfactory, Needs Improvement); P/F (Pass/Fail); A, B, C, D, F; and so on.
- Use each inner box of the grid to identify the criteria necessary to demonstrate

competence at each of the designated performance levels.

A rubric for the pre/post writing assessment strategy for the overhand throw illustrating the previously listed guidelines is included in Table 3.1 on page 21. Use this as an example for developing your own assessment rubrics.

Give students a copy of the scoring rubric before assessing them. This practice helps students

- know what is expected for reaching each performance level,
- become more personally responsible for meeting the best performance level they can, and
- use the rubric as a self-assessment tool, for self-feedback during a teacher-completed assessment, or for independent practice of the skill.

A pre-established rubric helps you as well by

- reducing the time required to score the assessment,
- facilitating communication with students, parents, and other teachers, and
- guiding parents and colleagues who want to reinforce the skills you're teaching and who wish to monitor students' progress after further practice.

Thus, parents and administrators should also receive copies of scoring rubrics used in your program.

Lesson-Level Worksheet Scoring Box

The scoring box is a method for recording student assessment data. The lesson-level worksheets in this book already contain a scoring box at the bottom of the page. This box contains a list of components the student may be assessed on during that lesson or unit. Typically, you will find a minimum of three areas: critical elements, concept quiz, and independent working skills.

Critical Elements

These criteria deal with the actual performance of the important parts of the skill being taught that class period. My scoring rubric for the critical elements utilizes the concepts of George Graham's Levels of Skill Proficiency presented in Children Moving (p. 40). Students using the critical elements in one or more of characteristics of the Proficiency Level earn five points. Students using the critical elements meeting one or more characteristics of the Utilization Level earn four points. Students using the critical elements meeting one or more characteristics of the Control Level earn three points. Students using the critical elements meeting one or more characteristics of the Precontrol Level earn two points. Students not meeting any characteristics of the Precontrol Level but participating in the activity earn one point.

Decide which critical elements are important for the students to master. You will find assessment objectives and teaching tips with each worksheet to guide you. Feel free to substitute information based on your program. These criteria focus on the psychomotor domain.

The alternative assessment concepts include critical elements and movement concepts. Movement concepts differ from critical elements in that they provide experiences in the quality of utilizing the critical elements that enhance the development of psychomotor skills.

Concept Quiz

In addition to demonstrating their ability to use the critical elements of a skill, I assess the students' understanding of the concepts related to the skill. Developmentally a student may not be able to demonstrate the skill at a proficient level; however, he or she may understand the concepts related to the skill. These criteria focus on the cognitive domain. The rubric used for scoring cognitive domain assessment strategies is as follows:

- Full credit (usually one point per answer) for answers that clearly identify correct response, provides accurate information and requires no interpretation on the part of the scorer.

- Partial credit (usually half credit per answer) for answers that require justification with verbal explanation/clarification from the student or interpretation on the part of the scorer.

I would recommend assessing either the psychomotor domain or the cognitive domain in the initial stages of assessing student learning. Assessing both domains initially will overwhelm the teacher and the students. Also, scoring the cognitive domain is somewhat easier (i.e., scoring does not have to occur in the real-time, so the teacher can reflect on the student responses) when starting to implement student assessment.

Independent Working Skills

Students need to develop the skills necessary for lifelong learning. The lifelong learner is able to work alone and with others, search out solutions, and stay focused on a task. I have found the work by Don Hellison to be appropriate for establishing criteria for assessing this area. I've modified the five levels he describes to meet the needs of the elementary children I teach. I strongly recommend that you read Hellison's book before implementing this strategy. These criteria focus on the affective domain.

The Level System

At the beginning of the school year, introduce your students to the level system and provide them with appropriate examples of behaviors that exemplify the level. With younger children it is helpful to have an example for each of the levels in the context of a class situation.

At the end of the class period, you, each student, or both of you identify the level of behavior the student demonstrated the majority of the class period. If you wish, you can assign points to each of the levels and use this as assessment data.

Independent Working Skills Model

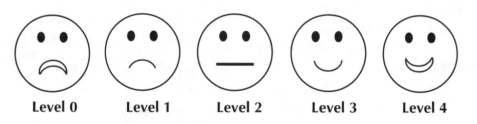

| Level 0 | Level 1 | Level 2 | Level 3 | Level 4 |

Level 0   *Double frown*—The student exhibits behaviors that prevent him or her, as well as others, from learning. Abusive behaviors fit in this category.

Level 1   *Single frown*—The student exhibits behaviors that prevent him or her from learning but does not interfere with the learning of the other students. Simply not participating and refusing to participate belong in this category.

Level 2   *So-so*—At times the student exhibits behaviors that are off-task. Child needs frequent reminders to stay focused on his or her work.

Level 3   *Single smile*—The student exhibits behaviors that are focused on the task and works continually without intervention by the teacher.

Level 4   *Double smile*—The student exhibits behaviors that are focused on the task, works continually without intervention by the teacher, *and* is helpful to classmates as needed.

Keeping Track of Assessment Data

To keep track of lesson-level assessment data use a daily assessment record sheet. Each class period requires a new sheet.

In the example provided, the top of the record sheet contains an area for the date and a brief notation on the critical element (or objective, desired outcome, or standard) presented in the lesson. The students in the class are listed on the sheet by learning teams (squads). Under each name, three letters (P, C, A) represent the three domains (psychomotor, cognitive, and affective) that you might assess during the learning episode. There is also room for brief reflective notes on students.

You can create a daily assessment record sheet template that fits your needs by hand or with a word processing program. Either way, make copies for future use. However, using a computer does offer a few advantages:

1. Computers produce more professional-looking record sheets.

2. You can print record sheets as needed.

3. You can save record sheet templates on disc, allowing you to revise data (e.g., adding or deleting student names) more efficiently throughout the school year.

The data from the daily assessment record sheets give you a concise source of information necessary for planning the next lesson. Indeed, this method serves as an organized method for keeping track of student skill, knowledge, and behavior data for each lesson and is therefore a powerful documentation tool.

In addition to lesson-level assessment data, you should establish an organized method for tracking and reviewing assessment data from a series of lessons, or unit. Using data from several lessons is critical in accurately evaluating student performance. Once again, you can organize data by hand or with the aid of a computer. To help you with hand recording, many teacher plan books include a record-keeping section for summarizing assessment data. The main advantage of using a computerized spreadsheet or grade management software program is the time saved in performing all the mathematical computations. In addition, computer grade management software programs offer features that sort assessment data by activity (P, C, or A) or score, develop histograms, show hypothetical predictions of assessment data, track student attendance, develop biographical cards on students, and make grade changes after retesting.

Tracking assessment data for large numbers of students can be overwhelming. As you begin, be selective in the type and amount of data you wish to keep track of for the purpose of assessing and evaluating student performance. The following tips should help you keep your sanity in tracking student assessment data:

- Use a computer as much as possible.
- Be selective in which data you track.
- Be organized.
- Be consistent (that is, don't change your system every week).
- Spend time every week entering and reflecting on assessment data collected.

Assessment Data Reports

Reviewing a class's overall assessment scores helps validate the assessment. Many computer programs can take raw scores and print a histogram, which is a means for graphically representing a frequency distribution. With a histogram, the physical educator can easily see the number of students scoring within a specific range on an assessment item.

Assessment and the Affective Domain

Developmentally appropriate physical education programs provide students with opportunities to develop psychomotor, cognitive, and affective skills. Throughout this book you will find a variety of methods for assessing student development in the psychomotor and cognitive domains. The affective domain deals with students' values, attitudes, and behaviors, making this a very challenging domain to assess objectively.

There are, however, observable skills and behaviors that provide insight into a student's affective development. In my physical education program, I've identified several essential skills and behaviors and labeled these as "Independent Working Skills." Independent Working Skills require students to demonstrate self-control, positive sportperson behaviors, and respect for others and equipment. Following directions and rules, playing under control, choosing equipment safely and quickly, working with and showing respect for a partner, helping less skilled classmates willingly, encouraging and complimenting others, sharing, and working together for a com-

mon goal are all examples of Independent Working Skills.

As with the cognitive and psychomotor domains, prior to assessing student development in the affective domain, the physical educator must provide appropriate educational experiences so students can learn and practice these skills. An effective strategy for accomplishing this task is to

- identify an observable affective skill or behavior for the class to focus on,
- provide examples of acceptable and unacceptable ways to use the skill or behavior,
- have students practice the acceptable uses of the skill or behavior, and
- observe students using the skill or behavior acceptably (or unacceptably) during the lesson.

As you begin to assess the affective domain skills or behaviors, you will need to tell the students which skill or behavior you are assessing. For each lesson, you might choose to assess a different affective skill or behavior. As the students become experienced in using the skills and behaviors you are fostering, you

---

How Will Your Progress Be Evaluated in Physical Education Class?

Your progress will be evaluated based on your development in the following areas:

Performance of Motor Skills (Psychomotor Domain)

Each class I will observe your development in the skill or skills you are learning. Everyone has different past experiences with the skills presented in class. Based on your experience level, I may observe the critical elements of the movement in isolation (one critical element at a time), in combinations (two or more critical elements at a time), or in an authentic situation (used in an activity).

Understanding of Movement Concepts (Cognitive Domain)

You will be asked to share your understanding of the movement concepts or critical elements of the skill you are learning about in class. You can demonstrate your understanding of concepts on a class quiz, pre- and postwrite opportunity, oral question-and-answer session, or homework assignment.

Self- and Social Responsibility (Affective Domain)

Each class I will observe your ability to demonstrate self-control, show respect for others and equipment, and use positive sportperson behaviors.

may wish to observe a particular affective skill or behavior unannounced. Ideally, affective domain assessment should occur every lesson, providing you with formative evaluation data to use for the evaluation (grading) process.

Using Assessment Data for Evaluating (Grading) Student Performance

Using assessment data for the purpose of evaluation (grading) is often perceived by administrators, parents, and students as the most important reason to assess student learning. You may be required to submit an evaluation related to student performance at the end of a nine-week period or a semester. The reporting system used for this evaluation is usually established by the school district and may use a traditional format such as numeric or letter grades, or a nontraditional

format such as a developmental checklist or narrative.

It is important that parents and students are aware of the role assessment (quizzes, pre- and postwrite, homework) plays in your evaluation of student performance. You should provide the information relevant to evaluating student performance at the beginning of the school year in the form of a physical education newsletter and/or handbook. The sidebar is a sample that I use in my newsletter and handbook.

Frequent assessment of student achievement based on well-designed assessment strategies provides the data necessary to determine competence in the skills, concepts, and behaviors you have presented in class. At the end of the nine weeks or semester, you can summarize lesson-level and other alternative and authentic assessment data into any number of evaluation reporting systems, depending on what your district requires.

Table 3.1 Scoring Rubric—Overhand Throw

Critical components	Level of performance			
	Highly exceeds Standard (A)	**Exceeds Standard (B)**	**Meets Standard (C)**	**Substandard (D)**
1. **Discipline specific terminology.**	Uses sport specific terminology when answering (i.e., opposition, trunk rotation, follow-through, etc.)	Uses combinations of sport specific and general descriptive terms when answering (i.e., opposite foot front, turn the trunk, etc.)	Uses general descriptive terms when answering (i.e., one foot in front, side to target, stretch to target, etc.)	Uses inaccurate terms when answering.
2. **Identifies correct critical elements.**	Identifies 7 or more critical elements.	Identifies 6 critical elements.	Identifies 5 critical elements.	Identifies less than 5 critical elements.
3. **Appropriate use of remediation and enrichment activities.**	• Lists a remediation and enrichment activity for 3 different factors (i.e., equipment, environment, accuracy, etc.). • Uses separate example for each remediation and enrichment activity.	• Lists a remediation and enrichment activity for 2 different factors. • Uses converse example for each remediation and enrichment activity (i.e., large ball and small ball).	• Lists a remediation and an enrichment activity. • Remediation and enrichment example may or may not relate to the same factor.	• Lists a remediation or an enrichment activity but not both.

Chapter 4

What About Student Portfolios?

Educators across the United States are examining the role of student portfolios in assessing student learning. Student *portfolios* serve as a collection site for student work and reflections on their work as they achieve class, school district, and/or state-level standards. Student portfolios can be

- subject specific or a collection of student work from all subject areas,
- graded as a whole or individual works contained in the portfolio can be graded, and/or

- used to collect student work for a specific time (e.g., semester, school year) or for the entire school career of the student.

There are two types of student portfolios: the *working portfolio* and the *cumulative portfolio*. Concepts for a working portfolio will be covered in this chapter. (Chapter 8 explains cumulative portfolios.) The working portfolio provides the day-to-day information important to student learning. Quizzes, worksheets, learning logs, and skill sheets are examples of working portfolio entries. In fact, any of the sample assessments in this book can be used as working portfolio entries. A working portfolio should also include entries that reflect student learning before and after instruction. Two strategies currently being used by physical educators include the following:

- Pre/post writes—students share "how-to" knowledge, attitudes, and personal reflections related to a skill at the beginning and end of a unit of study.
- Pre/post videotapes—students are videotaped performing designated skills at the beginning of the school year and then at the end of the school year. This strategy works well with individual motor skills or movement sequences and routines.

Managing portfolios for hundreds of students requires special treatment. After experimenting with several methods, I prefer to use double-pocket file folders. As a student enters my physical education program, I give him or her a pocket folder with his or her name on the outside of the folder. Each student uses the same folder for the entire elementary school experience.

I designate each pocket in the folder for a specific purpose. Materials that will be retained from year to year are filed on the inside left pocket. At the close of each school year, all the saved materials are stapled together, creating a packet of the student's work representing that school year. By the end of the elementary school experience, each child will have six packets of information from which to assess his or her own growth and development.

The pocket on the right side of the folder serves as a holding area for works in progress,

record sheets, pre/post writings, and skill sheets. Some of the information found on this side of the folder will be moved to the left pocket for permanent keeping; some of the information will be taken home by the student. In addition, you might choose to attach a third pocket to the back of the folder. This pocket can hold worksheets, homework papers, or additional information that the student should take home (e.g., program newsletters).

If you are unable to use double-pocket folders for your student portfolios, you may wish to use file folders or construction paper folders (use large sheets of paper folded in half and stapled on the sides). Both these methods work well as a collection site for one year; however, because they lack pockets to help hold papers in place, they do not work well for collecting materials for several years.

At the beginning of the school year, you can arrange the portfolios by homerooms or by class schedule. You can keep portfolios in an expandable folder or in the box that the portfolio folders came in (this works well when the student has little information in the folder). It is much easier to file entries in an organized set of portfolios.

There are several strategies available for filing information in the students' portfolios: have the student file his or her own information, have student helpers file information at various times in the school day, recruit parent volunteers for filing information, or use student interns.

Start slowly when initiating student portfolios. If you become overwhelmed in the beginning, you will not be motivated to continue with student portfolios. Some teachers begin to establish student portfolios with the incoming kindergarten class; then

You may find that your students already have portfolios in the classroom. Speak with the classroom teacher as to the possibility of the students' placing work from physical education class in their classroom portfolios. This could save you valuable storage space.

each school year, they add a new class. By starting with one grade level at a time, you'll have time to explore the concepts involved in a working portfolio while growing into a full-fledged school-wide portfolio system.

Chapter 5

Assessment Worksheets

The worksheets presented in this chapter assess student knowledge of fundamental movement concepts and skills appropriate for use with children in the primary grades. In addition, I have included several higher level assessment worksheets that require the student to differentiate between appropriate and inappropriate critical elements of skill performance. In order to appropriately assess nonreaders, many of the worksheets require the student to only recognize the concept or skill from a picture.

The format of this chapter closely follows the delivery of curriculum content in the Bloomsburg (Pennsylvania) Area School District. This format is highly effective for a physical education program meeting one day a week. Fundamental concepts and skills are presented in a logical, progressive manner, because competence in both nonlocomotor and locomotor skills is important for success in manipulative skills. For example, the skill of kicking requires competence in the nonlocomotor skills of bending, stretching, swinging, and pulling and the locomotor skill of leaping.

To help students learn the assessment process, resist the temptation to discuss more than one assessment item each turn. Give instructions and have students answer only one assessment item each turn. If you feel it would be helpful for a particular student or class, cut and paste only one item onto a clean sheet of paper and use this in isolation from the other assessment items on the worksheet I've provided.

How to Use the Assessment Worksheets

You will notice that the assessment worksheets in Part II reflect the Knowledge Level of Blooms Taxonomy. On the front of each page is a reproducible assessment worksheet. The back of each assessment worksheet provides information in the areas of Alternative Assessment concepts, Instructions for Implementation, and Teacher Tips.

Alternative Assessment Concepts

Not only would it be impossible to design an assessment worksheet which included every concept for each motor skill; it would be impossible to design assessments that reflected the critical elements you will highlight when you present the skill. This section, Alternative Assessment Concepts, allows you to customize any assessment worksheet to meet the needs of your program. Prior to designing your assessment, review the list of assessment concepts and then select those that are appropriate for your program.

Instructions for Implementation

Provided in this section you will find a brief listing (short reminder cues) of implementation strategies based on the listing provided in the Teacher Guide. Keep in mind when you first introduce an assessment strategy you should model the instructions for your students; this should help reduce confusion.

Teacher Tips

Teacher-friendly tips are shared in this section. All of these tips resulted from my own experiences in implementing the assessment strategy. It is always easier to learn from the experiences of another.

Teacher Guide for Chapter V Assessment Worksheets

The Teacher Guide provides specific information about the various assessment strategies found in chapter 5. This section is divided by topics (General Instructions, Student Instructions, FYIs, and Scoring Suggestions) so that the teacher can quickly find topic-related information.

General Instructions—a list of implementation strategies appropriate for any assessment strategy in chapter 5.

Student Instructions—teacher delivered instructions to the students participating in the assessment.

- **FYIs**—identifies important support skills/knowledge the student needs to participate successfully in the assessment strategy. Suggestions are also provided to increase or decrease the degree of difficulty for each assessment strategy.
- **Scoring Suggestions**—a method for scoring the various components of each assessment strategy is provided.

General Instructions

- Provide instructions orally for children.
- Complete a practice example with the entire class if necessary.
- Read each assessment item aloud for the class. This is important for nonreaders and auditory learners.
- Allow for *think time* and then read the item aloud again. The concept of *think time* provides children with time to process information. "Think time" is an important concept for children to practice. Allow for at least 15–30 seconds of *think time*.

- Encourage children to perform the movement or use visualization in order to recall information. The skills of problem solving, critical thinking, and movement analysis are incorporated in both techniques.
- Reread information as requested by children.
- Play an audio tape of the assessment worksheet so you will be *free* to monitor the class and provide assistance.

Student Instructions

The following section highlights the student instructions, FYI tips, and scoring suggestions for each assessment strategy.

Assessment Strategy—Circle the Answer (pages 32–51)

Student instructions: Draw a circle around the picture showing a _____.

(You may wish to use other methods for selecting the correct response such as an X or a smile face).

FYI

- Make sure all children in the class have mastered shape/letter recognition and basic handwriting skills prior to implementing this assessment strategy.
- Change the shape (square, rectangle, diamond) when the students have mastered the circle.
- To increase the difficulty of this strategy generate two questions for the assessment worksheet. Students will place a circle around the correct response for the first question and place an X on the correct response for the second question.

Scoring Suggestions

Full credit for the following:

- Selected response clearly illustrates the correct skill/critical elements
- appropriate use of designated strategy (i.e., circle around the picture)

- full name on assessment worksheet

Partial credit for the following:

- selected responses can be justified with a verbal explanation/clarification from the student
- not using designated response selection strategy (i.e., using an X instead of a circle to indicate the correct answer)
- first name only on the assessment worksheet

No credit for the following:

- response selected clearly incorrect
- not using any designated response selection strategy
- no name on assessment worksheet

Assessment Strategy—Labeling (pages 52–69)

Student instructions: Print the label (using a letter or a word) at the appropriate response.

FYI

- Make sure all children in the class have mastered letter recognition and basic handwriting skills for the letters/words needed for the assessment strategy.
- Identify where you want the student to label the answer. Should the label be placed beside, under, or on the appropriate response.
- Remember young children have LARGE handwriting. Allow sufficient room on the paper to accommodate LARGE handwriting.
- To increase the difficulty of this strategy challenge students to use the appropriate word for the label instead of just using a single letter to represent the label.
- Providing a word list can alleviate the need for correct spelling or allow students to use any of the temporary spelling strategies such as practice spelling or inventive spelling used by novice spellers.

Scoring Suggestions

Full credit for the following:

- label clearly identifies the correct response
- appropriate use of designated response selection strategy (label appears beside correct response)
- full name on assessment worksheet

Partial credit for the following:

- selected response can be justified with a verbal explanation/clarification from the student
- not using the designated response strategy (i.e., not placing a label in the appropriate area or using an inappropriate label)
- first name only on assessment worksheet

No credit for the following:

- response selected is clearly incorrect
- not using any designated response selection strategy
- no name on assessment worksheet

Assessment Strategy: True–False

(pages 70–85)

Student instructions: Draw a smile face in the circle if the statement is right. Draw a frown face in the circle if the statement is wrong.

FYI

- When using this strategy for the first time place two dots representing "eyes" in the circle so the child will only have to draw a smile or a frown.
- Children enjoy adding hair/jewelry/glasses to their circle face. This will keep the children who finish "first" involved while waiting for the other children to complete the assessment worksheet.
- Children with advanced skills could be challenged to identify the incorrect part of the statement.

Scoring Suggestions

Full credit for the following:

- selected response correctly identifies statement as true or false.

- appropriate use of designated selection strategy (smile for true and frown for false)
- full name on assessment worksheet

Partial credit for the following:

- selected response can be justified with a verbal explanation/clarification from the student
- not using designated response selection strategy (i.e., using a half smile for a frown face or a straight face)
- first name only on assessment worksheet

No credit for the following:

- response selected clearly incorrect
- not using any designated response selection strategy
- no name on assessment worksheet

Assessment Strategy: Oral Quiz

(pages 92–101)

This strategy can be used to assess knowledge level information quickly at the end of a learning episode. Additional benefits for using an oral quiz format in the physical education program include.

1. You can tailor the questions to reflect the critical elements covered in the actual learning episode.
2. You can use terminology appropriate to the students in each class.
3. If student does not understand an assessment item you can immediately rephrase the item.
4. Less material intensive. Most short answer quizzes will fit on a quarter sheet of paper.

Student Instructions: Number your paper from 1 to (how many answers/questions you may have on the quiz). Listen to the question and then write/illustrate your answer.

FYI

- Limit your questions; two or three questions are sufficient.
- Use the same terminology that you used in the lesson.
- Focus the items on the critical information presented in the learning episode.

Sample Oral Quiz Questions:

- Name the skill we focused on today in class.
- List the critical elements of the skill we focused on today.
- What cues could you check to improve a friend's performance. You may use cues from previous lessons.
- List one critical element from today's skill you use well.
- List one critical element from today's skills you do not use well.

Scoring Suggestions

Full credit for the following:

- response provides accurate information related to the question
- response requires no interpretation on the part of the scorer
- full name on quiz

Partial credit for the following:

- response can be justified with a verbal explanation/clarification from the student
- some interpretation of the response is required on the part of the scorer
- first name only on the quiz

No credit for the following:

- response clearly incorrect
- no name on the quiz

CRITICAL ELEMENTS OF BASIC SHAPES

Alternative Assessment Objective

The child will demonstrate the ability to recognize shapes the body can make.

Teacher Tips

- You may wish to assess only one basic shape concept at a time. Simply cut and paste this sample assessment worksheet onto a clean sheet of paper to tailor this to your class's needs.

Extensions

- Include other shapes (e.g., oval and diamond).
- Clip pictures of people performing movement activities that make other shapes from magazines (or take pictures of students making shapes with the body), mount on tagboard, and have children identify the shapes as a class or at a station on a circuit. Additional examples include forward roll (circle) and ready position for a dive (straight).
- Depending on the ability of your students, use as a guided small-group practice sheet instead of as an assessment tool.

Teacher Notes:

BASIC SHAPES

Blue   **Green**   **Red**   **Yellow**

Circle the picture of the child using their body to make a:

1. Triangle

2. Rectangle

3. Square

Full name _____

Color group _____

Concept quiz _____

Independent working skills _____

CRITICAL ELEMENTS OF LEVELS IN ACTION

Alternative Assessment Objective

The child will demonstrate the ability to recognize and identify movement at various levels.

Teacher Tips

- You may wish to assess only one level at a time. Simply cut and paste this sample assessment worksheet onto a clean sheet of paper to tailor this to your students' needs and abilities.

Extensions

- Design an assessment sheet that uses sport-related visuals and have children identify the level of the skill or movement, for example, a football player in a three-point stance (medium level) or a dancer on point (high level).

- Have partners explore ways to move smoothly from a low, to a medium, then to a high level.

Teacher Notes:

LEVELS IN ACTION

NAME _____ DATE _____

| Blue | Green | Red | Yellow |

For each picture, circle the name of the level the child is moving in:

1. Low   Medium   High

2. Low   Medium   High

3. Low   Medium   High

4. Low   Medium   High

5. Low   Medium   High

Critical elements _____

Full name _____

Concept quiz _____

Independent working skills _____

CRITICAL ELEMENTS OF WALKING

Alternative Assessment Objective

The child will demonstrate the ability to recognize and identify the locomotor skill of walking.

Teacher Tips

- Remind the students to look at the action of the feet.

Extensions

- Introduce or review the basic critical elements of walking:

    Transfer of weight from one foot to the other.

    One foot is always in contact with the floor.

- Introduce the role that the following movement concepts have on the quality of the walk:

    Directions: forward, backward, left side, right side.

    Speed: slow, medium, fast.

- Have the students give an example of when they use the skill of walking.

Teacher Notes:

LOCOMOTOR SKILLS—WALK, JUMP, OR GALLOP?

NAME _____ DATE _____

Blue   **Green**   **Red**   **Yellow**

Circle the word that shows the movement this child is using:

Walk   **Jump**   **Gallop**

Full name _____

Color group _____

Concept quiz _____

Independent working skills _____

CRITICAL ELEMENTS OF RUNNING

Alternative Assessment Objective

The child will demonstrate the ability to recognize and identify the locomotor skill of running.

Teacher Tips

- Remind students to look at the action of the feet.

Extensions

- Introduce or review the basic critical elements of running:

    There is a point at which both feet are off the ground.

    Involves oppositional movement of the arms and legs.

    Bend the elbows and swing the arms.

    Keep knees up.

    Push off from the balls of the feet.

- Introduce the role that the following movement concepts have on the quality of the run:

    Pathways: straight, curved, zigzag

- Have the students give an example of when they use the skill of running.

Teacher Notes:

LOCOMOTOR SKILLS—SLIDE, RUN, OR HOP?

NAME _____ DATE _____

Blue   **Green**   **Red**   **Yellow**

Circle the word that shows the movement this child is using:

Slide   **Run**   **Hop**

Full name _____

Color group _____

Concept quiz _____

Independent working skills _____

CRITICAL ELEMENTS OF JUMPING

Alternative Assessment Objective

The child will demonstrate the ability to recognize and identify the locomotor skill of jumping.

Teacher Tips

- Remind students to look at the action of the feet.

Extensions

- Introduce or review the basic critical elements of jumping:

  Use an upward arm lift.

  Explode upward.

  All body parts must work together.

  Use the arms to jump higher.

  Use a two-footed takeoff and a two-footed landing.

  Coordinate the movements of the arms and legs.

  Crouch your body as knees bend.

  Land softly (bend hips, knees, and ankles to absorb shock).

- Introduce the role that the following movement concepts have on the quality of the jump:

  Ranges: near, far.

  Levels: high, medium, low.

- Have the students give an example of when they use the skill of jumping.

Teacher Notes:

LOCOMOTOR SKILLS—HOP, SLIDE, OR JUMP?

NAME _____ DATE _____

Blue   **Green**   **Red**   **Yellow**

Circle the word that shows the movement this child is using:

_____

Hop   **Slide**   **Jump**

Full name _____

Color group _____

Concept quiz _____

Independent working skills _____

Reproduced by permission from Suzann Schiemer's *Assessment Strategies for Elementary Physical Education* (Human Kinetics 2000).

CRITICAL ELEMENTS OF HOPPING

Alternative Assessment Objective

The child will demonstrate the ability to recognize and identify the locomotor skill of hopping.

Teacher Tips

- Remind students to look at the action of the feet.

Extensions

- Introduce or review the basic critical elements of hopping:

    Push off and land on the same foot.

    Lift arms as you spring up.

    Use arms at the sides for balance.

    Land softly (bend knees and ankles to absorb shock).

- Introduce the role that the following movement concepts have on the quality of the hop:

    Ranges: near, far.

    Levels: high, medium, low.

- Have the students give an example of when they use the skill of hopping.

Teacher Notes:

LOCOMOTOR SKILLS—HOP, SLIDE, OR JUMP?

NAME _____ DATE _____

| Blue | Green | Red | Yellow |

Circle the word that shows the movement this child is using:

Hop   **Slide**   **Jump**

Full name _____

Color group _____

Concept quiz _____

Independent working skills _____

CRITICAL ELEMENTS OF LEAPING

Alternative Assessment Objective

The child will demonstrate the ability to recognize and identify the locomotor skill of leaping.

Teacher Tips

- Remind students to look at the action of the feet.

Extensions

- Introduce or review the basic critical elements of leaping:

    Involves oppositional movement of the arms and legs.

    There is a point at which both feet are off the floor and the legs are stretched apart in a stride position.

    When you leap you are in the air longer than when you jump.

    Take off from one foot and land on the other foot.

- Introduce the role that the following movement concepts have on the leap:

    Directions: forward, backward.

    Levels: high, medium, low.

- Have the students give an example of when they use the skill of leaping.

Teacher Notes:

LOCOMOTOR SKILLS—SKIP, LEAP, OR RUN?

NAME _____ DATE _____

Blue   Green   Red   Yellow

Circle the word that shows the movement this child is using:

_____

Skip   Leap   Run

Full name _____

Color group _____

Concept quiz _____

Independent working skills _____

CRITICAL ELEMENTS OF GALLOPING

Alternative Assessment Objective

The child will demonstrate the ability to recognize and identify the locomotor skill of galloping.

Teacher Tips

- Remind students to look at the action of the feet.

Extensions

- Introduce or review the basic critical elements of galloping:

    Step and draw the back foot to the front foot.

    Move forward or backward.

    Bend knees.

    Stay on the balls of the feet.

- Introduce the role that the following movement concepts have on the gallop.

    Directions: forward, backward.

    Speed: slow, medium, fast.

- Have the students give an example of when they use the skill of galloping.

Teacher Notes:

LOCOMOTOR SKILLS—GALLOP, LEAP, OR SLIDE?

NAME _____ DATE _____

| Blue | Green | Red | Yellow |

Circle the word that shows the movement this child is using:

Gallop   **Leap**   **Slide**

Full name _____

Color group _____

Concept quiz _____

Independent working skills _____

CRITICAL ELEMENTS OF SLIDING

Alternative Assessment Objective

The child will demonstrate the ability to recognize and identify the locomotor skill of sliding.

Teacher Tips

- Remind students to look at the action of the feet.

Extensions

- Introduce or review the basic critical elements of sliding:
    - Step and draw the back foot to the front foot.
    - Move in a sideways direction (left or right).
    - Bend knees.
    - Stay on the balls of the feet.
- Introduce the role that the following movement concepts have on sliding.
    - Directions: right side, left side.
    - Levels: low, medium, high.
- Have the students give an example of when they use the skill of sliding.

Teacher Notes:

LOCOMOTOR SKILLS—SKIP, SLIDE, OR WALK?

NAME _____ DATE _____

Blue   **Green**   **Red**   **Yellow**

Circle the word that shows the movement this child is using:

Skip   **Slide**   **Walk**

Full name _____

Color group _____

Concept quiz _____

Independent working skills _____

CRITICAL ELEMENTS OF SKIPPING

Alternative Assessment Objective

The child will demonstrate the ability to recognize and identify the locomotor skill of skipping.

Teacher Tips

- Remind students to look closely at the action of the feet.

Extensions

- Introduce or review the basic critical elements of skipping:

    Step forward, then hop up on the same foot.

    Alternate feet.

    Lift knees up.

    The arm swing is upward in time with the legs.

- Introduce the role that the following movement concepts have on skipping.

    Directions: forward, backward.

    Pathways: straight, curved, zig zag.

- Have the students give an example of when they use the skill of skipping.

Teacher Notes:

LOCOMOTOR SKILLS—JUMP, RUN, OR SKIP?

NAME _____ DATE _____

Blue   **Green**   **Red**   **Yellow**

Circle the word that shows the movement this child is using:

Jump   **Run**   **Skip**

Full name _____

Color group _____

Concept quiz _____

Independent working skills _____

Reproduced by permission from Suzann Schiemer's *Assessment Strategies for Elementary Physical Education* (Human Kinetics 2000).

CRITICAL ELEMENTS OF LEVELS

Alternative Assessment Objective

The child will demonstrate the ability to recognize and identify levels of the body in space.

Teacher Tips

- Write the letters "H," "M," and "L" on a chalkboard or flip chart for students to refer to when completing the assessment.
- Note that this is an introductory-level quiz designed for children who are just beginning to explore the concept of levels. Remember to keep initial assessment strategies simple so that the children are not unnecessarily confused by the assessment strategy. Higher level assessment strategies for the concept of levels are provided on the following pages.

Extensions

- Have small groups of students explore more activities that put the body at each of the levels.
- Have students in small groups identify each other's levels.
- Low Level
    - Belly Crawl
    - Log Roll
    - Seal Walk
    - Sitting on the floor and moving forward or backward.
- Medium Level
    - Crawling
    - Knee Walk
    - Puppy Walk (walk using hands and feet—belly facing the floor)
    - Crab Walk
- High Level
    - Locomotor Skills
    - Grapevine Step
    - March
    - Shuffle

Teacher Notes:

NAME _____ DATE _____

Blue   **Green**   **Red**   **Yellow**

Use the picture to show me the three levels we used in today's class. Put a letter "H" on the body at the high level, put a letter "M" on the body for medium level, and put a letter "L" on the body for low level.

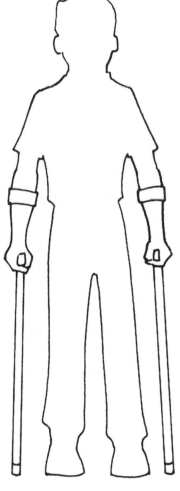

Critical elements _____

Full name _____

Concept quiz _____

Independent working skills _____

CRITICAL ELEMENTS OF BEND AND STRETCH

Alternative Assessment Objective

The child will demonstrate the ability to recognize and identify the nonlocomotor movements of stretching and bending.

Teacher Tips

- When giving instructions, emphasize that students should label the picture showing the *best* example of the movement requested.

Extensions

- Identify or review the critical elements of bending:

    The body part becomes shorter or smaller (think of "folding" the body).

    Two body parts become closer together.

    Occurs at the joints of the body.

    Is a *drawing in* toward the body.

    May also be called *flexing*.

- Identify or review the critical elements of stretching:

    The body part becomes longer or straighter.

    The body part extends as the joints straighten out.

    Movement is away from the center of the body.

    May also be called *extension*.

    Often used as a warm-up or cool-down exercise.

- Point out that these two skills are opposite actions.

- Brainstorm a list of some everyday activities and sport skills that use bending and stretching.

- List other action words and dance terms that would describe these two movements.

- Relate how flexibility training enhances these skills.

Teacher Notes:

NONLOCOMOTOR SKILLS—BEND AND STRETCH

NAME _____ DATE _____

| Blue | Green | Red | Yellow |

S = on the child who is showing a lot of **stretching**.
B = on the child who is showing a lot of **bending**.

Full name _____

Color group _____

Concept quiz _____

Independent working skills _____

CRITICAL ELEMENTS OF PUSH AND PULL

Alternative Assessment Objective

The child will demonstrate the ability to recognize and identify the nonlocomotor movements of pushing and pulling.

Teacher Tips

- When giving instructions, emphasize that students should label the picture showing the *best* example of the movement requested.

Extensions

- Introduce or review the critical elements of pushing:

  Press against an object to make it move.

  Movement is away from the body.

  Start with a bend and move to a stretch as you are pushing.

- Introduce or review the critical elements of pulling:

  Dragging the object to make it move.

  Movement is toward the body.

  Start with a stretch and move to a bend as you are pulling an object.

- Note that these two skills are opposites.
- Brainstorm a list of some everyday activities and sport skills that use pushing and pulling.
- List other action words and dance terms that describe these two movements.

Teacher Notes:

NONLOCOMOTOR SKILLS—PUSH AND PULL

NAME _____ DATE _____

| Blue | Green | Red | Yellow |

O = around the child who is showing **pushing**.
X = on the child who is showing **pulling**.

Full name _____

Color group _____

Concept quiz _____

Independent working skills _____

CRITICAL ELEMENTS OF SHAKE AND STRAIN

Alternative Assessment Objective

The child will demonstrate the ability to recognize and identify the nonlocomotor skills of shaking and straining.

Teacher Tips

- Remember, resist the temptation to discuss both assessment items at the same time. Give instructions and have students answer only one assessment item at a time.

Extensions

- Introduce or review the critical elements of shaking:

    Involves back-and-forth movement.

    Move quickly.

- Introduce or review the critical elements of straining:

    Make the body or body part hard, tight, and tense.

    Sometimes called *tension*.

- Note that these two skills are opposites.
- Brainstorm a list of some everyday activities and sport skills that use shaking and straining.
- List other action words and dance terms that would describe these two movements.

Teacher Notes:

NONLOCOMOTOR SKILLS—SHAKE AND STRAIN

NAME _____ DATE _____

| Blue | Green | Red | Yellow |

X = on the child who is showing **shaking**.
O = around the child who is showing **straining**.

Full name _____

Color group _____

Concept quiz _____

Independent working skills _____

CRITICAL ELEMENTS OF SWING AND SWAY

Authentic Assessment Objectives

The child will demonstrate the ability to recognize and identify the nonlocomotor skills of swinging and swaying.

Teacher Tips

- Remember, give instructions and have students answer only one assessment item at a time.
- Before doing any formal assessment of these two terms, make sure students have extra practice in telling the difference between them, as they are often used interchangeably in other disciplines.

Extensions

- Introduce or review the critical elements of swinging:

    Involves freer movement backward and forward than swaying does.

    Body part may move in an arc or a circle.

    Involves a pendular movement.

    Movement is less controlled than in swaying.

- Introduce or review the critical elements of swaying:

    Involves more restricted side-to-side movement, as opposed to the backward and forward movement of swinging.

    Transfer weight (shift) from one body part to another body part.

    Involves more controlled shifting of body weight than in swinging.

- Brainstorm a list of some things you see in the world around you that swing and sway.
- List sport skills that use swinging and swaying.
- List other action words and dance terms that describe these two movements.

Teacher Notes:

NONLOCOMOTOR SKILLS—SWING AND SWAY

NAME _____ DATE _____

Blue   **Green**   **Red**   **Yellow**

O = around the child who is **swinging** an object.
X = on the child who is **swaying** an object.

Full name _____

Color group _____

Concept quiz _____

Independent working skills _____

CRITICAL ELEMENTS OF TWIST AND TURN

Alternative Assessment Objective

The child will demonstrate the ability to recognize and identify the nonlocomotor skills of twisting and turning.

Teacher Tips

- Demonstrate the movements with a prop (towel or scarf) or other object to review the terms before you assess them.
- Remember, only one assessment item at a time.

Extensions

- Introduce or review the critical elements of twisting:

  Rotate a part of the body at a joint.

  There is a limit to how far you can twist because one end of the twisting part is bound (can't move freely).

- Introduce or review the critical elements of turning:

  Movement changes the direction of the body or a part of the body.

  You end up facing a new direction.

  Involves shifting body weight.

  Both ends of the body part or body are free to move.

- Brainstorm a list of some everyday activities and sport skills that use twisting and turning.

- List other action words and dance terms that describe these two movements.

- Give students scarves they can practice twisting and turning. Have partners analyze each other's scarf movements.

Teacher Notes:

NONLOCOMOTOR SKILLS—TWIST AND TURN

NAME _____ DATE _____

Blue	**Green**	**Red**	**Yellow**

O = around the child who is showing **twisting**.
X = on the child who is showing **turning**.

Full name _____

Color group _____

Concept quiz _____

Independent working skills _____

Alternative Assessment Objective

The child will demonstrate the ability to recognize and identify several nonlocomotor skills, distinguishing one from another.

Teacher Tips

- This assessment works best with students experienced in simpler written assessments. For younger or less experienced students, you can divide this material into four separate assessments by cutting this worksheet into four pieces.

- Remember, make sure students can read the word choices offered so you're assessing their physical education knowledge instead of their reading abilities.

Extensions

- Brainstorm a list of everyday activities that involve combinations of nonlocomotor skills. Help the children identify those combinations.

- Have the students draw pictures of the everyday activities the class discussed.

Teacher Notes:

NONLOCOMOTOR COMBINATIONS IN PHYSICAL ACTIVITY

NAME _____ DATE _____

Blue	Green	Red	Yellow

Bend	Twist	Swing	Push	Stretch
Turn	Sway	Pull	Shake	Strain

List the nonlocomotor skill or skills used in each of the pictures. Write the word by the body part using that skill or skills. Use the words in the box above to help you.

1.

3.

2.

4.

Full name _____

Color group _____

Concept quiz _____

Independent working skills _____

CRITICAL ELEMENTS OF WALKING

Alternative Assessment Objective

The child will demonstrate the ability to recognize and identify the locomotor skill of walking.

Teacher Tips

- Remind the students to look at the action of the feet.

Extensions

- Have students work in pairs to identify the critical elements of their partner's walking.

Teacher Notes:

LOCOMOTOR SKILLS—WALKING

NAME _____ DATE _____

| Blue | Green | Red | Yellow |

W = on the child who is **walking**.

Full name _____

Color group _____

Concept quiz _____

Independent working skills _____

Reproduced by permission from Suzann Schiemer's *Assessment Strategies for Elementary Physical Education* (Human Kinetics 2000).

CRITICAL ELEMENTS OF WALKING AND RUNNING

Alternative Assessment Objective

The child will demonstrate the ability to distinguish the locomotor skill of walking from the locomotor skill of running.

Teacher Tips

- Remind the students to look at the action of the feet.

Extensions

- Review the critical elements of walking.
- Review the critical elements of running.

Teacher Notes:

LOCOMOTOR SKILLS—WALKING AND RUNNING

NAME _____ DATE _____

Blue **Green** **Red** **Yellow**

W = on the child who is **walking**.
R = on the child who is **running**.

Full name _____

Color group _____

Concept quiz _____

Independent working skills _____

CRITICAL ELEMENTS OF HORIZONTAL JUMPS

Alternative Assessment Objective

Recognize the critical elements of the horizontal jump.

Teacher Tips

- Emphasize the critical elements in the lesson.
- Make sure students know that a smile face means "true" and a frown face means "false."

Extensions

- Give students one or two of the following hints at a time to help them improve their horizontal jumps:

    Swing your arms back and then forward.

    Push off with two feet.

    Bend your knees before jumping and on the landing.

    Swing your arms in the direction of the jump.

    Stretch and reach forward.

    Land on two feet at the same time.

    Reach forward on the landing.

    On the pushoff, the toes will leave the floor last.

    On the landing, the heels will touch the floor first.

    Crouch your body on takeoff.

    Land softly (bend hips, knees, and ankles).

- Point out how this skill requires coordinating the arms and legs.
- Explain and demonstrate that an even rhythm pattern is essential for this skill.
- Brainstorm a list of which activities, games, and sports use the skill of jumping far. Some examples to get you started include:

    Track and field

    Long jump

    Gymnastics

Teacher Notes:

JUMPING FAR—HORIZONTAL JUMPS

NAME _____ DATE _____

| **Blue** | **Green** | **Red** | **Yellow** |

Draw a smile face for True.
Draw a frown face for False.

Swing your arms back and then forward when jumping far.

Push off the floor with two feet.

Stretch and reach up when you are jumping far.

Keep your legs straight when you land.

Critical elements of jumping far _____

(Takeoff, flight, landing)

Full name _____

Concept quiz _____

Independent working skills _____

CRITICAL ELEMENTS OF VERTICAL JUMPS

Alternative Assessment Objective

The child will demonstrate understanding of how to increase vertical jump height.

Teacher Tips

• Make sure the students know that a smile face means "true" and a frown face means "false."

Extensions

• Give students one or two of the following hints at a time to help them improve their vertical jumps:

Swing arms up.

Explode upward.

All body parts must work together.

Use a two-footed takeoff and a two-footed landing.

Coordinate the movements of the arms and legs.

Crouch your body on takeoff.

Land softly.

• Brainstorm a list of which activities, games, and sports use the vertical jump. Some examples to get you started include:

Basketball

Volleyball

Soccer

Track and field

Diving

Ice skating

Cheerleading

Chinese jumprope

Teacher Notes:

JUMPING HIGH—VERTICAL JUMPS

NAME _____ DATE _____

Blue   **Green**   **Red**   **Yellow**

Draw a smile face for True.
Draw a frown face for False.

You should bend your knees before you jump high.

You should land on two feet.

Your body should be stretched when you are in the air.

To jump high you should keep your arms down.

Critical elements of jumping high _____

(Takeoff, flight, landing)

Full name _____

Concept quiz _____

Independent working skills _____

CRITICAL ELEMENTS OF LANDING SAFELY

Alternative Assessment Objective

The child will demonstrate understanding of how to improve safe landings.

Teacher Tips

- Make sure the students know that a smile face means "true" and a frown face means "false."

Extensions

- Introduce or review the critical elements of safe landings:

    Use arms for balance.

    Land with feet shoulder-width apart.

    Give upon impact in the ankles, knees, and hips.

    Do not land flat-footed.

    Remember to land softly.

- Brainstorm a list of which activities, games, and sports use the skill of landing safely. Some examples to get you started include:

    Gymnastics

    Basketball

    Volleyball

    Ski (snow and water) jumping

    Parachuting

Teacher Notes:

LANDING SAFELY

NAME _____ DATE _____

| Blue | Green | Red | Yellow |

Draw a smile face for True.
Draw a frown face for False.

Your feet should be touching each other when you land.

You should use your arms for balance when you land.

Keep your legs straight when you land.

Your legs should "give" when your feet touch the floor.

Critical elements of landing safely _____

(Balance, foot placement, give)

Full name _____

Concept quiz _____

Independent working skills _____

CRITICAL ELEMENTS OF HOPPING

Alternative Assessment Objective

The child will demonstrate the ability to identify some of the critical elements of hopping.

Teacher Tips

- Make sure the students know that a smile face means "true" and a frown face means "false."

Extensions

- Review the critical elements of hopping:

  Land on the ball of your foot.

  Hop using the left and then the right foot.

  Lift your arms as you spring up.

  Push off from the toes.

  Use your arms at the sides for balance if necessary.

  Land softly.

- Explain that this skill is an even rhythm pattern.
- Brainstorm a list of which activities, games, and sports use the skill of hopping.

  Hopscotch

  Track and field—Triple jump

  Diving

  Gymnastics

Teacher Notes:

NAME _____ DATE _____

| **Blue** | **Green** | **Red** | **Yellow** |

Draw a smile face for True.
Draw a frown face for False.

You should take off and land on the same foot.

Your hopping foot should leave the floor.

When you land, your foot should make a loud noise.

You need good balance to hop.

Critical elements of hopping _____

(Takeoff, flight, landing)

Full name _____

Concept quiz _____

Independent working skills _____

CRITICAL ELEMENTS OF LEAPING

Alternative Assessment Objective

The child will demonstrate the ability to identify some of the critical elements of leaping.

Teacher Tips

- Make sure the students know that a smile face means "true" and a frown face means "false."

Extensions

- Review the critical elements of leaping:

  Use arms in opposition to legs.

  Do not land flat-footed.

  To push off, push up and forward with the rear foot.

  Lead with either leg.

  Keep head up.

  Lean forward.

  Like the run, there is a point at which both feet are off the floor, but with leaping you are in the air longer.

  Take off from one foot and land on the other foot.

  The force of the pushoff determines the distance and height of the leap.

  Stretch the legs during the flight.

  The landing leg needs to bend when the foot touches the floor.

  Land softly.

- Brainstorm a list of activities, games, and sports that use leaping. Some examples to get you started include:

  Dance

  Gymnastics

  Track and field (Shotput, Discus)

  Rhythmic gymnastics

Teacher Notes:

LEAPING

NAME _____ DATE _____

| Blue | Green | Red | Yellow |

Draw a smile face for True.
Draw a frown face for False.

You can use a leap to go over objects.

Your forward leg should stretch when you leap.

You push off and land on the same foot.

You should push off on your forward foot.

Critical elements of leaping _____

(Push, stretch, one-footed landing)

Full name _____

Concept quiz _____

Independent working skills _____

CRITICAL ELEMENTS OF SLIDING

Alternative Assessment Objective

The child will demonstrate the ability to identify some of the critical elements of sliding.

Teacher Tips

- Make sure the students know that a smile face means "true" and a frown face means "false."

Extensions

- Review the critical elements of sliding:

   One foot leads, and the other follows behind.

   Step to the side and draw the back foot (following foot) to the front foot (leading foot).

   Do not slide flat-footed; stay on the balls of the feet.

   Keep knees bent slightly.

   Lean forward slightly.

- Explain that this skill is an uneven rhythm pattern.

- With older or more experienced students, compare the rhythm pattern of sliding (uneven) to that of hopping (even).

- Brainstorm a list of activities, games, and sports that use the skill of sliding. Some examples to get you started include:

   Tennis

   Basketball

   Baseball—fielding and infield ball lead off base

Teacher Notes:

SLIDING

Blue　　　　　**Green**　　　　　**Red**　　　　　**Yellow**

Draw a smile face for True.
Draw a frown face for False.

One foot is the leader when you slide.

You can slide to the right side or to the left side.

Your legs should cross when you slide.

Sliding and galloping move in the same direction.

Critical elements of sliding _____

(one foot leading, bent knees, ride on ball of foot)

Full name _____

Concept quiz _____

Independent working skills _____

CRITICAL ELEMENTS OF SKIPPING

Alternative Assessment Objective

The child will demonstrate the ability to identify some of the critical elements of skipping.

Teacher Tips

• Make sure the students know that a smile face means "true" and a frown face means "false."

Extensions

• Review the critical elements of skipping:

Step forward, then hop up on the same foot.

Do the same with the other foot.

Keep knees up.

This is a combination of two movements: stepping and hopping.

The arm swing is upward in time with the legs.

• Explain that this skill uses an uneven rhythm pattern.

• Brainstorm a list of activities, games, and sports that use the skill of skipping. Some examples to get you started include:

Folk dance

Teacher Notes:

NAME _____ DATE _____

| **Blue** | **Green** | **Red** | **Yellow** |

Draw a smile facc for True.
Draw a frown face for False.

Each foot gets to be the leader when you skip.

The leader foot does two things: step and hop.

You should land on the back part of your foot when you skip.

Skipping can move in more than one direction.

Critical elements of skipping _____

(Step, hop, alternating feet, knee lift, land on ball of foot)

Full name _____

Concept quiz _____

Independent working skills _____

CRITICAL ELEMENTS OF DODGING

Alternative Assessment Objective

The child will demonstrate the ability to identify some of the critical elements of dodging.

Teacher Tips

- Make sure the students know that a smile face means "true" and a frown face means "false."

Extensions

- Review the critical elements of dodging:

    Stay balanced.

    Change directions and speeds quickly.

    Move away from an object or a person.

    Dodging can be stationary or on the move.

    Dodging helps us move safely.

- Brainstorm a list of activities, games, and sports that use the skill of dodging. Some examples to get you started include:

    Football

    Fencing

    Tag

    Wrestling

    Soccer

- List other action words that describe dodging. Some examples to get you started include:

    Keep away

    Fake, move quickly and change direction

Teacher Notes:

DODGING

	Blue	**Green**	**Red**	**Yellow**

Draw a smile face for True.
Draw a frown face for False.

Use a dodge to keep from bumping into other students.

When you dodge you change directions.

You move slowly when you dodge.

Are you good at dodging?

Critrical elements of dodging _____

(Quick, change direction, look)

Full name _____

Concept quiz _____

Independent working skills _____

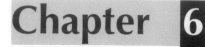

Chapter 6

Assessing With Alternative and Authentic Strategies

We can now explore alternative and authentic assessments that require multiple lessons to complete. You can also use pieces of these assessments as lesson-level assessments. The worksheets provide the students with an opportunity to experience alternative assessment strategies. The unit-level assessments provide an opportunity to experience authentic assessment. Initially, you may find alternative and authentic assessment to be overwhelming. However, with experience you will recognize the important role alternative and authentic assessment play in measuring student learning.

General Instructions

Follow these suggestions to get the most out of each worksheet:

- Provide instructions orally for children.

- Complete a practice example with the entire class if necessary.

- Read each assessment item aloud for the class. This is important for nonreaders and auditory learners.

- Allow for "think time," and then read the assessment item aloud again. This provides the children with time to process information. Children need to practice thinking before responding.

- Allow students to respond with drawings. When using this strategy encourage the students to label each illustration.

- Reread information as requested by children.

- Tape record assessment worksheets and play the audiotape for the children. This frees you to monitor the class and provide assistance.

Overview of Alternative Assessment Strategies

The four alternative assessment strategies—prewrite and postwrite, critical elements, self-reflection, and self-assessment—require students to use higher order thinking skills: problem solving and critical and creative thinking. Assessment areas include manipulative skills, fitness education, cooperation, and self-recording. Although the four strategies can work as stand alone lessons independently, they work best as multilesson (unit) assessments. Multilesson assessments require students to demonstrate an ability to apply information learned from a variety of opportunities. Because they dig deeper, these assessments require two or more class periods for the student to complete the assessment. (This is as opposed to stand-alone assessments measuring the knowledge presented and learning acquired in a single class period; the student is not required to build upon knowledge from previous lessons in order to successfully complete the assessment.)

Pre- and Postwrite (pages 92–98)

Asking students to write about a skill or activity at the beginning of a unit can give you insights about student knowledge, experience, and attitudes toward the skill or activity. Completing a unit of study with a postwriting activity then allows you to measure student growth in conceptual knowledge, terminology, application of the skill, and enjoyment of the skill or activity.

During the first lesson of the unit, ask students to complete the prewrite, encouraging them to share what they know about the skill before you begin instruction. It is acceptable for students to answer, "I don't know." Use this baseline data to assess student learning at the end of the unit.

Have students complete the postwrite at the end of the unit—using the same questions found on the prewrite. Compare the postwrite to the prewrite for each student to measure the cognitive and affective growth of the student.

I begin using this strategy with children in second grade. Note that the information requested becomes more complex as the child progresses from second to fifth grade. This encourages students to develop the skills necessary to become a physically educated person. These skills include self-assessment of skill ability, basic understanding of skill mechanics and terminology, recognition of games and activities that use the skill, ability to select remediation and enrichment activities when appropriate, and identification of skills they find enjoyable. These skills help a child learn in all three domains: cognitive, affective, and psychomotor.

Beginning on page 90, I have provided sample writing sheets, each with a skill identified (underhand and overhand throw, strike, and volley). Then I offer two blank writing sheets for you to fill in with skills appropriate for your program.

Critical Elements of Fitness Items
(pages 102–107)

This assessment strategy requires students to learn the correct form (critical elements) of a fitness assessment item, use peer assessment strategies to evaluate performance, and use the skill in challenge activities and practice tests. Initially it will take approximately two lessons to complete this assessment strategy. However, as the students learn the format and protocols, they will need less time when using other fitness items. The fitness items used in this section are from Physical Best's *FITNESSGRAM* (backsaver sit and reach, push-up, and curl-up); however, you can substitute other assessment items. Direct students to complete the activities on each assessment worksheet in order, so that these assessment tools become teaching tools as students practice test techniques and the process of self-assessment.

- As we learn more about assessing health-related fitness, be aware that the critical elements for the various assessment items may change. The format I've provided is designed so that you can readily add and delete information as critical elements change.

- Provide oral instructions for the first activity on the assessment sheet.

- Provide a visual model of the critical elements for the fitness item. A teacher demonstration is especially effective.

- Introduce the instructions for the Challenge sections. Be prepared to provide these instructions again when the students reach that section.

- Scoring suggestions—As the students are engaged in the worksheet, you can observe individual student technique while they perform the assessment items; then you can provide individual assistance.

Give full credit for demonstrating all the critical elements.

Give partial credit for missing one or two critical elements in the demonstration.

Assign no credit for missing more than two critical elements in the demonstration.

Self-Reflection (pages 108–109)

This self-assessment strategy encourages students to reflect on their own learning.

Melograno (1998) explains that students "can reflect on how they learn and why they fail to learn. Students can also engage in a self-assessment of their . . . relative growth in targeted areas, strengths and weaknesses, and short-term and long-term goals." Thus, providing time to reflect is an important part of authentic assessment, and reflection assessments are essential to well-rounded student portfolios.

Direct students completing the reflection assessment (page 109) to provide the information requested for each question or statement based on his or her participation in the cooperative activity. Tell them to complete the worksheet section by section—activity, then reflection, activity, then reflection. Keep in mind that the assessment items require the student to provide short answers. You may wish to establish a time frame for each assessment item so that students will pace themselves and lost instructional time will be minimized.

Develop a scoring rubric that reflects the following critical components:

- completion of worksheet
- quality of reflections
- use of proper sentence formation (only if required by your administration or in cooperation with the teacher responsible for teaching written language)
- other aspects of your program, such as use of terminology found in cooperative ventures, reflections on how to improve cooperative choices, and improvement shown in working cooperatively.

You should *not* score students on the accuracy of the self-reflection or the values expressed in the reflections.

Self-Recording (pages 110–111)

This strategy is designed to teach students how to record their own performance scores accurately and then use that information for reflection and self-assessment. To use this strategy, tell students that following each practice trial, they will score their perfor-

mances. If they successfully used the critical elements (or made the distance, hit the target, or the like) they will draw a smile in the circle. If they are unsuccessful in an attempt, they will draw a star in the circle. The star represents the fact that they made an unsuccessful attempt and honestly recorded the results.

It is essential to encourage honest reporting in self-assessments. To do this, you must make it safe for the student to be honest. Therefore, rather than punishing the student for not being successful, reward the student for unsuccessful attempts and for honestly recording an appropriate score. For example, the worksheet on self-recording (page 111) directs the students to record a star for unsuccessful attempts as a reward for trying. Have students analyze how they're doing in words, or record what their goals are in the "Thinking About Learning" section.

- Students may respond using illustrations in the "Thinking About Learning" sections. When using this strategy encourage the students to label their illustrations.
- While the students are engaged in completing the assessment worksheet, you could observe individual skill technique and provide individual assistance.
- Have students tabulate the number of stars and smiles. Keep in mind that stars and smiles must be of equal value. If you make one symbol more valuable than the other you will encourage grade inflation (cheating, lying).

Combining Alternative Assessment Strategies

The assessment strategies of pre- and postwrite, critical elements, self-reflection, and self-assessment are advanced-level assessment strategies that require instruction and practice time for students to become proficient at them. The pre- and postwrite asks students to provide information on a variety of topics such as skill analysis, remediation and enrichment, and skill application. The critical element assessment sheet focuses on the skills of peer assessment of the essential elements of a skill in a variety of situations. The self-reflection assessment sheet provides the student with an opportunity to monitor his or her behaviors and provide a short narrative on the decision-making process from among the behavior choices. The self-assessment sheet requires students to keep an accurate record of their abilities to use the critical elements of a skill or skill performance factors (e.g., distance, accuracy). Only introduce one new strategy in a class period. Otherwise, students may become overloaded or confused with the various assessment requirements.

After the students have successfully explored and experienced each assessment strategy separately, you may then opt to combine two or more strategies. A combination I have found very effective is to use pre- and postwrite, critical elements, and self-assessment. For example, at the beginning of the instructional unit or theme, I use the prewrite to collect student information relevant to the upcoming skill. As the students begin to focus on learning and practicing the critical elements of the skills, I find the critical element assessment sheet to be an important learning and assessment tool. Then I use the self-assessment sheet during skill practice. At the completion of the instructional unit or theme, I have the students complete the postwrite to assess conceptual knowledge learned during the unit or theme. The data collected from these multiple assessment strategies provides a comprehensive view of individual student achievement and development.

CRITICAL ELEMENTS OF THE UNDERHAND THROW

Alternative Assessment Objective

The student will demonstrate knowledge of how to throw underhand and will self-assess own underhand throwing ability and attitude.

Teaching Tips

- Question 1—Child rates ability to use the manipulative skill by circling the word that best matches his or her perception of his or her skill ability.
- Question 2—Child shares knowledge about how to perform the skill. Look for appropriate terminology and conceptual understanding.
- Question 3—The child shares information regarding how well he or she enjoys performing the skill by circling the word or phrase that best matches his or her level of enjoyment.

Extensions

- Underhand Throw

  Opposite foot in front.

  Pendulum Swing

  Body weight shifts forward.

  Follow through in direction of the target.

  The backswing and the follow through add force to the throw.

Teacher Notes:

UNDERHAND THROW

NAME _____ DATE _____

Blue	**Green**	**Red**	**Yellow**

1. Can you throw underhand?

    Yes   Sort of   No

2. Tell me how to throw underhand:

3. Do you like to throw underhand?

    Yes   Sort of   No

Reproduced by permission from Suzann Schiemer's *Assessment Strategies for Elementary Physical Education* (Human Kinetics 2000).

CRITICAL ELEMENTS OF THE OVERHAND THROW

Alternative Assessment Objective

The student will demonstrate knowledge of how to throw overhand and will self-assess own overhand throwing ability and attitude.

Teaching Tips

- Question 5—Child shares knowledge of games that use the skill. (This is a great method for relating fundamental manipulative skills to sport-specific skills.)

Extensions

- Overhand Throw

    Step out with the opposite foot.

    Side to target.

    Ball close to the ear on throwing side.

    Segmental rotation.

    Body weight shifts forward.

    Elbow of throwing arm leads forward.

    Follow through in direction of the target.

    The backswing and the follow through add force to the throw.

Teacher Notes:

OVERHAND THROW

NAME _____ DATE _____

Blue	**Green**	**Red**	**Yellow**

1. Rate your ability to throw overhand.

Semipro	Need more practice	Just learning	Never tried it

2. Tell me how to throw an object using an overhand motion:

3. How could you make throwing an object overhand easier to do?

4. How could you make throwing an object overhand harder to do?

5. List any games, sports, and physical activities that use the skill of overhand throwing that you can think of:

6. Do you like to throw an object using an overhand motion?

Yes	Sort of	No	I don't know

CRITICAL ELEMENTS OF THE HORIZONTAL STRIKE

Alternative Assessment Objective

The student will demonstrate knowledge of how to strike sidearm and will self-assess own sidearm striking ability and attitude.

Teaching Tips

- Questions 3 and 4—Child shares knowledge about remediation and enrichment activities related to the skill. (Remember, the physically educated person possesses the knowledge to modify a skill.)

Extensions

Eyes on the ball/object.

Opposite foot in front.

Side to the target.

Level Swing

Segmental rotation

Body weight shifts forward.

Follow through in direction of the target.

The backswing and the follow through add force to the strike.

Teacher Notes:

HORIZONTAL STRIKE

NAME _____ **DATE** _____

Blue	**Green**	**Red**	**Yellow**

1. Can you hit (strike) an object using a sidearm swing?

    Yes   Sort of   No   I don't know

2. Tell me how to hit (strike) an object using a sidearm swing:

3. How could you make hitting (striking) an object sidearm easier?

4. How could you make hitting (striking) an object sidearm harder?

5. Do you like to hit (strike) an object with a sidearm swing?

    Yes   Sort of   No   I don't know

CRITICAL ELEMENTS OF THE VOLLEY

Alternative Assessment Objective

The student will demonstrate knowledge of how to volley and will self-assess own volleying ability and attitude.

Teaching Tips

- After the prewrite, have students brainstorm a list of words or phrases that could be used in place of the word *volley* or to help describe the skill (e.g., back and forth).

Extensions

Eyes on the ball/object.

Move to the ball/object.

Push the ball/object using the hands/racket.

Use a variety of striking patterns to volley an object (underhand, sidearm, and overhand).

Follow through in the direction of the target.

Teacher Notes:

VOLLEY

NAME _____ **DATE** _____

Blue	**Green**	**Red**	**Yellow**

1. Rate your ability to volley an object:

Semipro	Need more practice	Just learning	Never tried it

2. Tell me how to volley an object:

3. How could you make volleying an object easier to do?

4. How could you make volleying an object harder to do?

5. List any games, sports, and physical activities that use the skill of volleying:

6. Do you like to volley?

Yes	Sort of	No	I don't know

NAME _____ DATE _____

Blue	Green	Red	Yellow

Skill: _____

1. Can you _____?

Yes   Sort of   No

_____

2. Tell me how to _____?

_____

3. Do you like to _____?

Yes   Sort of   No

VOLLEY

NAME _____ DATE _____

| **Blue** | **Green** | **Red** | **Yellow** |

Skill: _____

1. Rate your ability to _____.

    Semipro   Need more practice   Just learning   Never tried it

2. Tell me how to _____:

3. How could you make _____ easier to do?

4. How could you make _____ harder to do?

5. List any games, sports, or physical activities that use the skill of _____:

6. Do you like to _____?

    Yes   Sort of   No   I don't know

CRITICAL ELEMENTS OF SIT-AND-REACH TEST

Alternative Assessment Objective

The child will demonstrate the ability to self- and peer assess correct sit-and-reach technique and will perform and record one practice test trial.

Teaching Tips

In Sections 2 and 3, students record scores for correct technique, not for ability to perform. A student earns one point for each part of the critical elements he or she can perform correctly. Explain that the critical elements listed at the top of this worksheet are for students to refer to throughout the rest of the assessment. In Section 4, students practice performing and recording the scores of an actual back saver sit-and-reach test.

Follow these more specific tips to get the most out of this worksheet:

Section 1: Important Parts of the Back Saver Sit-and-Reach Test

- To introduce this lesson, ask "The back saver sit-and-reach is the recommended test for flexibility of which area of the body?" (*Hamstring [back-of-thigh] muscles.*)

- Perform the test yourself and have the class practice assessing your back saver sit-and-reach technique using the critical elements listed.

- Help students identify incorrect movements during the back saver sit-and-reach:

    Knee of the extended leg bent

    One hand reaching forward farther than the other hand

    Turning the body away from the testing box

    Keeping both legs straight

    Movement not smooth

- Emphasize safe stretching techniques: Move slowly and smoothly, no bouncing or jerking!

Section 2: Practice One Back Saver Sit-and-Reach Test

- Let students work at their own pace.

- Remind students to use the blanks to record the score of the sit-and-reach critical elements. Each critical element area is worth one point (each assessment sheet contains four critical element areas). If the child successfully completes all the critical element areas he or she earns a 4 (four points), if the child is unsuccessful in one of the critical element areas he or she earns a 3 (three points), and so on.

- Have partners alternate turns.

Section 3: How Far Can You Reach?

- Students challenge themselves to perform their best sit-and-reach. On the fourth reach, they record the score on the assessment sheet (no score will be recorded for a poor performance).

- Remind children to use both the right and left legs.

- Each student tries to meet or exceed his or her previous score on each succeeding turn.

- Partners alternate turns.

Section 4: Sit-and-Reach Practice Test

- Give students the opportunity to self-test the back saver sit-and-reach (using, for example, *FITNESSGRAM*).

THE BACK SAVER SIT-AND-REACH TEST 1

NAME _____ DATE _____

| **Blue** | **Green** | **Red** | **Yellow** |

Section 1: Important Parts of the Back Saver Sit-and-Reach Test

Any time you perform an actual back saver sit-and-reach test, you will follow these steps using each leg four times. You will record your score for each leg for the fourth try only. Today, in Sections 2 and 3, your partner will give you one point for each step you do correctly. In Section 4, you will practice performing an actual back saver sit-and-reach test. Remember to take off your shoes!

_____ Leg position: One leg straight with foot flat against the end face of the test box. The other leg is bent at the knee and the bottom of the foot is flat on the floor, to the side of the knee of the straight leg.

_____ Arm position: Arms are straight with one hand on top of the other. Arms are stretched over the measuring stick.

_____ Reach position: With palms down, stretch forward from the waist with both hands. Do four times. *Caution:* Move slowly and steadily to the point of discomfort—not pain! No bouncing!

_____ Hold position: Hold the fourth stretch for at least one second (count "1,001").

Section 2: Practice One Back Saver Sit-and-Reach Test

Practice one back saver sit-and-reach on each leg. Show your partner good form. Record your scores by giving yourself one point for each of the four correct parts (critical elements) each try. Maximum score for each try is four points.

1. _____   2. _____   3. _____   4. _____   5. _____   6. _____

Section 3: How Far Can You Reach?

Your scores (record distance on measuring stick—incorrect technique will result in no score):

   Right ____   Left ____   Right ____   Left ____

Section 4: Back Saver Sit-and-Reach Practice Test

   Test your partner on the back saver sit-and-reach. Remember to use good form and test both legs.

   Your score (record to the nearest inch):

   Right _____   Left _____

CRITICAL ELEMENTS OF THE PUSH-UP

Alternative Assessment Objective

The child will demonstrate the ability to self- and peer assess correct push-up technique and will perform and record one practice test trial.

Teaching Tips

To introduce this lesson ask students, "The push-up is the recommended test for strength and endurance of which area of the body?" (*Upper body.*) Remember, make sure students know that in Sections 2 and 3, students record scores for correct technique, not for ability to perform. A student earns one point for each part of the critical elements he or she can perform correctly. Explain that the critical elements listed at the top of this worksheet are for students to refer to throughout the rest of the assessment. Then in Section 4, students practice performing and recording how many push-ups they can perform.

Follow these more specific tips to get the most out of this worksheet:

Section 1: Important Parts of the Push-Up

- Perform a push-up yourself and have the class practice assessing your push-up technique, using the critical elements listed.

- Help students identify incorrect movements during the push-up:

    Parts of the body other than hands and toes touching the floor

    Back swayed

    Body piked in the middle (at the hips)

    Arms not bent 90 degrees on the down position

    Arms not fully straightened during the up position

    Movement not smooth

Section 2: Practice One Push-Up

- Let students work at their own pace to complete this section. Remind students that each critical element area is worth one point. Partners should take turns.

Section 3: How Many Can You Do?

- Partner A performs as many quality push-ups as possible. When he or she stops, the score is recorded on the assessment sheet (push-ups using poor technique should not be counted). Then Partner B performs. Partner A will try to meet or exceed his or her previous score on the next turn. Partners A and B alternate turns.

Section 4: Push-Up Practice Test

- Give students the opportunity to self-test the push-up using a cadence cassette (e.g., from *FITNESSGRAM*).

THE PUSH-UP TEST

NAME _____ DATE _____

| Blue | Green | Red | Yellow |

Section 1: Important Parts of the Push-Up

Any time you perform an actual push-up test, you will follow these steps. Today, in Sections 2 and 3, your partner will give you one point for each step you do correctly. In Section 4, you will practice performing an actual push-up test.

_____ Hand position: Hands under shoulders with fingers spread apart.

_____ Body up position: Arms are straight. Back and legs straight (straight from head to toes).

_____ Body down position: Bend elbows 90 degrees (like the corner of a square) to lower the body. Upper arms parallel to (flat as) the floor. Body straight.

_____ Repeat: Return to body up position (arms straight). Continue alternating body up position and body down position.

Section 2: Practice One Push-Up

Practice one push-up. Show your partner good form. Record your scores by giving yourself one point for each of the four correct parts (critical elements) of each try. Maximum score for each try is four points.

1._____   2._____   3._____   4._____   5._____   6._____

Section 3: Challenge 1: How Many Can You Do ?

Partner will stop you when you do not show correct form.

1. _____   2. _____   3. _____

Section 4: Challenge 2: Push-Up Practice Test

Use the push-up cassette. How many push-ups can you do in time with the tape? Try to keep up with the beeps and use good form.
Your score:

1. _____   2. _____   3. _____

CRITICAL ELEMENTS OF THE CURL-UP

Alternative Assessment Objective

The child will demonstrate the ability to self- and peer assess correct curl-up technique and will perform and record one practice test trial.

Teaching Tips

To introduce this lesson ask students, "The curl-up is the recommended test for strength and endurance of which area of the body?" (*Abdominal muscles*.) Remember, make sure students know that in Sections 2 and 3, students record scores for correct technique, not for ability to perform. A student earns one point for each part of the critical elements he or she can perform correctly. Explain that the critical elements listed at the top of this worksheet are for students to refer to throughout the rest of the assessment. Then in Section 4, students practice performing and recording how many curl-ups they can perform.

Follow these more specific tips to get the most out of this worksheet:

Section 1: Important Parts of the Curl-Up

- Perform a curl-up yourself and have the class practice assessing your curl-up technique, using the critical elements listed.

- Help students identify incorrect movements during the curl-up:

    Feet or heels leaving the floor

    Bending the arms

    Using the hands to push the body up off the mat

    Not touching head to mat

    Movement not smooth

- Provide very specific instructions on how to place the measuring card correctly. The card should be under the performer's knees with the fingertips resting on the edge of the card. The partner should hold the card in place during the curl-ups. Because this is such an important part of this test, you might want to design a written or performance assessment through which you have children demonstrate their knowledge of measuring card placement.

- Divide students into groups of three. Explain each person's role: (1) test performer, (2) curl-up counter posted behind head of performer, and (3) measuring card holder. The three will rotate roles until each student has completed the worksheet.

Section 2: Practice One Curl-Up

- Let students work at their own pace to complete this section. Remind students that each critical element is worth one point. Partners should take turns.

Section 3: How Many Can You Do?

- Partner A performs as many quality curl-ups as possible. When he or she stops, the score is recorded on the assessment sheet (poorly performed curl-ups will result in stopping the performance and should not be counted). Then Partner B performs. Partner A will try to meet or exceed his or her previous score on the next turn. Partners A and B alternate turns.

Section 4: Curl-Up Practice Test

- Give students the opportunity to self-test the curl-up using a cadence cassette (e.g., from *FITNESSGRAM*).

Note: I have modified the *FITNESSGRAM* curl-up test to meet the needs of my students. See the *FITNESSGRAM Test Administration Manual* for specific protocols.

THE CURL-UP TEST

NAME _____ DATE _____

| Blue | Green | Red | Yellow |

Section 1: Important Parts of the Curl-Up

Any time you perform an actual curl-up test, you will follow these steps. Today, in Sections 2 and 3, your partner will give you one point for each step you do correctly. In Section 4, you will practice performing an actual curl-up test.

_____ Body down position: Lie on back with knees bent. Keep feet on floor. Arms straight with hands on mat (palms down).

_____ Curl-up position: Upper part of back curls up. Arms stay straight and fingers slide across the measuring card until fingertips reach the other side of the card. Keep feet flat on the floor.

_____ Curl-down position: Curl back down until the head touches the mat.

_____ Repeat: Alternate the curl-up and curl-down positions.

Section 2: Practice One Curl-Up

Practice one curl-up. Show your partner good form. Record your scores by giving yourself one point for each of the four correct parts (critical elements) of each try. Maximum score for each try is four points.

1. _____   2. _____   3. _____   4. _____   5. _____   6. _____

Section 3: How Many Can You Do?

Incorrect technique will stop the challenge.

1. _____   2. _____   3. _____

Section 4: Curl-up Practice Test

Use the curl-up cassette. How many curl-ups can you do in time with the tape? Try to keep up with the beeps and use good form.
Your score:

1. _____   2. _____   3. _____

Reproduced by permission from Suzann Schiemer's *Assessment Strategies for Elementary Physical Education* (Human Kinetics 2000).

CRITICAL ELEMENTS OF COOPERATION SELF-REFLECTION

Alternative Assessment Objective

The child will self-reflect on his or her ability to work cooperatively in a group.

Teaching Tips

During the lesson, have students participate in three or four cooperative activities. Following each activity, direct students to take a minute to identify how well they were able to cooperate and why they were successful or unsuccessful in demonstrating cooperation.

To enhance the chances of success, begin with cooperative activities that require a low level of motor skill and cooperative behavior. As the lesson progresses, include activities that require higher levels of motor skill and more complex cooperative behaviors.

- At the beginning of the lesson have the class generate a list of behaviors that demonstrate cooperation (see list on worksheet for ideas).

- As a group, select several behaviors the class will try to demonstrate in the activity portion of the lesson. Have students place a check mark by each targeted critical element on the worksheet.

- Classes having trouble with cooperation will need to focus on only one or two behaviors at a time, until they improve.

Teacher Notes:

COOPERATION SELF-REFLECTION

NAME _____ DATE _____

| Blue | Green | Red | Yellow |

Review the Critical Elements of Cooperation

_____ Follow rules.

_____ Help less-skilled classmates.

_____ Want everyone to play and succeed.

_____ Encourage others.

_____ Try hard to apply skills.

_____ Play under control.

_____ Compliment others.

_____ Control temper.

_____ Share.

_____ Show concern for classmates' feelings.

_____ Work together toward a common goal.

Activity 1: Rate yourself on your cooperative skills:

(lowest)   1 ____   2 ____   3 ____   4 ____   5 ____   (highest)

Why did you give yourself this rating?

_____

Activity 2: Rate yourself on your cooperative skills:

(lowest)   1 ____   2 ____   3 ____   4 ____   5 ____   (highest)

Why did you give yourself this rating?

_____

Activity 3: Rate yourself on your cooperative skills:

(lowest)   1 ____   2 ____   3 ____   4 ____   5 ____   (highest)

Why did you give yourself this rating?

_____

Activity 4: Rate yourself on your cooperative skills:

(lowest)   1 ____   2 ____   3 ____   4 ____   5 ____   (highest)

Why did you give yourself this rating?

CRITICAL ELEMENTS OF SELF-RECORDING

Alternative Assessment Objective

The child will demonstrate the ability to self- and peer assess and to work both independently and cooperatively.

Teaching Tips

This assessment worksheet allows you to monitor the number of practice trials a student makes during the designated time period.

- Explain that, beginning with circle number 1, students will score themselves or a partner on the designated task.

- A student should draw a smile face in the appropriate circle for each successful trial and a star if the attempt is unsuccessful. A star shows that the student has made an attempt and has recorded an honest response.

- At the end of the designated time, have students tabulate and review the smiles and stars they earned. Using the information on the record sheet, ask students to establish a realistic goal for the next class.

- In the "Thinking About Learning" section, students can write their goals or write about what they learned from the lesson. You could also have them use this area like a log or journal entry, eliminating the need for a separate journal or notebook.

- Using the scoring box:

    Critical elements—Score the student's use of the critical element(s) highlighted for that class. You may choose to use a separate rubric and enter it here.

    Independent working skills—Score the student's use of skills necessary to work independently.

    Worksheet score—Total number of trials, successful attempts, and unsuccessful attempts from the practice session.

    Concept knowledge—Score from quiz relevant to the knowledge of the terminology and critical elements presented in the lesson. You could give this quiz orally, and the students could answer on the back of the worksheet.

Teacher Notes:

SELF-RECORDING

NAME _____ DATE _____

| Blue | Green | Red | Yellow |

Skill or activity: _____

Draw a smile face if you do the skill right. Give yourself a star if you try but don't get the skill right.

1 ◯ 2 ◯ 3 ◯ 4 ◯ 5 ◯ 6 ◯

7 ◯ 8 ◯ 9 ◯ 10 ◯ 11 ◯ 12 ◯

13 ◯ 14 ◯ 15 ◯ 16 ◯ 17 ◯ 18 ◯

19 ◯ 20 ◯ 21 ◯ 22 ◯ 23 ◯ 24 ◯

25 ◯ 26 ◯ 27 ◯ 28 ◯ 29 ◯ 30 ◯

31 ◯ 32 ◯ 33 ◯ 34 ◯ 35 ◯ 36 ◯

Thinking About Learning:

Critical elements: _____

_____

Independent working skills: _____

_____

Worksheet score: _____

_____

Concept knowledge: _____

_____

Chapter 7

Project Assessments

The project assessments (goal setting and video project) found in this chapter require students to apply skills and concepts in practical ways. Like other strategies, you can use these strategies as a stand alone assessment; however, they work best as multilesson (unit) assessments. As discussed in chapter 6, multilesson assessments require students to demonstrate the ability to apply information they have learned in several lessons. In addition, projects may require students to complete assessment tasks outside of class. For example, they may need to research information, plan and design movement sequences, or practice movement skills and sequences.

This chapter uses a different format due to the depth of information required. Each unit-level assessment is introduced with a brief description of the assessment strategy: its uses, benefits, and goals. The educational theme and content assessed in this strategy

and the minimum number of classes needed for implementation are found here. The following sections appear in each lesson:

• Starting the lesson—Key concepts students must be familiar with in order to successfully participate in the lesson are featured here. It is necessary to review these concepts because of their importance and relevance to the assessment piece. This part prepares students to learn optimally from the rest of the lesson.

• Developing the lesson—Here concepts that serve as the focal point of the lesson are identified. In addition, you will find appropriate activities for applying and practicing the concepts.

• Ending the lesson—This section highlights important information you should review at the end of the lesson to reinforce learning. When appropriate, concepts important to the next lesson may also be introduced in this segment.

• Assessment worksheets—All the worksheets you need to carry out the assessment are provided.

A Self-Assessment Goal-Setting Project in Fitness Education

Quality health-related fitness education programs provide students with information related to the whys and hows of fitness concepts, testing, goal setting, and personal fitness plan development. The following thematic assessment is designed to help students use fitness test results for setting realistic goals and designing safe workout sessions to achieve the goals they have established.

This assessment strategy focuses on using data gathered from the PACER (*FITNESSGRAM*) test of aerobic fitness to establish aerobic fitness goals, work toward achieving the goals, and reflect on goal attainment.

In order for fitness test results to be valid, it is important that students learn how to perform the fitness test items proficiently (see practice sessions in chapter 6). In this section, you will find an assessment sheet designed to teach the critical elements of the PACER test. See pages 119-120 for assessment sheets designed for other fitness test items. The number of fitness assessment items you wish to include will determine the number of class periods needed to implement this assessment strategy. The following example focuses on goal setting for one fitness test item (the PACER test of aerobic fitness) and requires at least three class periods to implement. You can, however, assess any of the other health-related fitness components (flexibility, muscular strength and endurance, and body composition) with this strategy.

Lesson 1: Self-Assessment and Goal Setting

This lesson helps students learn about self-assessment, appropriate goal setting, and the relationship between these two aspects of a personal fitness plan. Students should have several chances to practice the format of this or any other health-related fitness test before self- or teacher assessment. Then they or you will be assessing ability, instead of familiarity with the test procedures.

Equipment Needed

> PACER audiotape
> Cassette player and sound system
> Marked course, 20 meters wide

Starting the Lesson

• Review the importance of using the critical elements for correct performance of the PACER aerobic fitness assessment. Explain that an incorrect performance yields invalid data.

• Introduce or review the concept of perceived exertion.

Developing the Lesson

• Provide an appropriate warm-up activity.

• Direct each student to participate in the PACER test.

• Provide an appropriate cool-down activity following the PACER test.

• Have students record their PACER test scores on the worksheet.

• Discuss the importance of using assessment data in setting goals.

- Discuss how to set realistic goals.
- Have students use the results from the PACER test to establish a personal fitness goal for aerobic endurance.

Closing the Lesson

- Review the role of physical activity in achieving fitness goals.
- Review FITT (frequency, intensity, type, and time) acronym.
- Announce retest date (the class period after next) for the PACER test.

Lesson 2: The Workout

This lesson helps students see the connection between fitness test scores, goals, and the work needed to improve their fitness levels.

Equipment Needed

Miniworkout station equipment for aerobic workout (e.g., jump ropes, steps, PACER audiotape, and tape player)

1 stopwatch per pair of students or easily visible clock with second hand

1 worksheet per student ("Did You Give Your Heart a Workout?" on pages following p. 109)

Pencils

Starting the Lesson

- Review personal goals established last class.
- Use the PACER activity, performed at half speed or so, as a segment of the warm-up.
- Introduce how important working out regularly is to meeting fitness goals.
- Introduce the use of the FITT concepts in designing a safe workout.
- Review information related to perceived exertion for heart rate, breathing, and general body information and the role this information has in designing a safe workout.

Developing the Lesson

Set up several miniworkout stations to create an aerobic workout, for example, rope jumping, PACER test practice, step aerobics, and the like.

- Working as partners, have students travel to the various miniworkout stations. Direct one partner to perform the activity while the other student times the workout with a stopwatch. Switch roles. Each student should perform for three minutes before moving on to the next station.
- Following each miniworkout, have students rate their perceived exertion on the worksheet, determining and recording the level of their workout. Remind students that the goal is to stay in a safe and effective workout zone.
- Discuss the effects of various physical activities on perceived exertion. For example: How did they respond to the different miniworkout activities? Why did some activities require more exertion than others?

- Discuss the role working out has in meeting goals. Relate to FITT concepts and the principles of overload and progression.
- Review progress toward goals, either through self-reflection or privately with the teacher.

Closing the Lesson

- Discuss the importance of working out outside of the physical education class in order to meet goals.
- Set up workout plan.

Lesson 3: Did You Achieve Your Goal?

This lesson helps students see the connection between working out and actually reaching goals.

Starting the Lesson

- Discuss the importance of honesty in recording results from the PACER test and honest reflection on the goal sheet.
- Review how working out regularly while applying the FITT, overload, and progression principles contributes to goal attainment.

Developing the Lesson

- Have students warm up prior to performing the PACER test.
- Have students perform the PACER test.
- Direct students to record their scores from the PACER test.
- Encourage students to reflect on their test results and to write a brief explanation as to why he or she did or did not attain the goal on the goal-setting worksheet.

Closing the Lesson

- Encourage students to share what they learned from participating in this thematic assessment.
- Place entire assessment packet in each student's portfolio.

PARTS OF THE PACER TEST OF AEROBIC ENDURANCE

PACER Test of Aerobic Endurance

_____ Move to the opposite line before the beep. When you step on the line, raise your hand.

_____ On the beep, turn and move back to the other line. No matter where you are, turn around on the beep.

_____ Continue traveling from line to line with the beep.

PACER Practice

Your score:

Smiles_____

Stars_____

PACER GOAL-SETTING WORKSHEET

NAME_____ DATE_____

1. Baseline Data: PACER Test of Aerobic Endurance

Write down your **score** for 21 laps of the PACER test.

Smiles _____   Stars_____   Date:

Reasons for your score:

Review your score on the PACER test. Write down a personal **goal** for 21 laps of the PACER test that you would like to meet by the end of the fitness education unit.

Smiles _____   Stars_____

What activities do you plan to include daily to help you achieve this goal?

_____

2. Practice Data: PACER Test of Aerobic Endurance

Write down your **score** for 21 laps of the PACER.

Smiles _____   Stars_____   Date:

Reasons for your score:

_____

3. Final Data: PACER Test of Aerobic Endurance

Write down your **score** for 21 laps of the PACER.

Smiles _____   Stars_____   Date:

Did you meet the goal you set above?   Yes   No

Why or why not?

Reproduced by permission from Suzann Schiemer's *Assessment Strategies for Elementary Physical Education* (Human Kinetics 2000).

NAME _____ DATE _____

Aerobic Workout Station 1: Jumping Rope

Jump rope for three (3) minutes (have your partner time you with a stopwatch). Rate yourself on the following categories immediately following your workout.

1. Sweating

Circle the best answer for you:

    None   A little   Quite a bit   A lot

2. Heartbeat

Circle the best answer for you:

    Usual pace   Quickly   Racing   Wobbly legs

3. Breathing

Circle the best answer for you:

Normally   Can hear yourself a little   Hard   Very hard   Out of breath

Look at your results for each of the categories. What level did you work out at?

    Too easy   Medium   Hard   Very hard   Too hard

Was this a good workout level for you today?   Yes   No

Why or why not? _____

Aerobic Workout Station 2: Walk or Jog

Walk or jog for three (3) minutes (have your partner time you with a stopwatch). Rate yourself on the following categories immediately following your workout.

1. Sweating

Circle the best answer for you:

    None   A little   Quite a bit A lot

2. Heartbeat

Circle the best answer for you:

    Usual pace   Quickly   Racing   Wobbly legs

3. Breathing

Circle the best answer for you:

    Normally   Can hear yourself a little   Hard   Very hard   Out of breath

Look at your results for each of the categories. What level did you work out at?

Too easy   Medium   Hard   Very hard   Too hard

Was this a good workout level for you today?   Yes   No

Why or why not? _____

In order to meet your PACER goal what will you have to do when you work out?

_____

A Video Project in Educational Gymnastics

Video assessment offers physical educators a method to capture real-time skill performance for future analysis and evaluation. You can use video technology to view one skill or a series of skills without worrying about being distracted during a crucial part of the performance. In addition, you can collect assessment data without losing your instructional time with the students. In fact, you can selectively tape skill performance in a real-world context, for example, a gymnastics lesson, martial arts practice, or at recess. In other words, you can observe a student actually applying the skill. Finally, the replay capabilities of your VCR will allow you to observe the same performance as many times as you need to. This will make it easier for you to see if the student has mastered the critical elements of the targeted movement skill.

The following assessment is an educational gymnastics video project that incorporates the themes of static and dynamic balance. Use the teaching technique of scaffolding to assist the students in developing the knowledge important to designing a static and dynamic balance sequence that meets the criteria of this project. In scaffolding, you communicate the relationship of concepts presented in past and future lessons or skill theme (Graham 1992). In other words, you help the students connect past, present, and future learning in meaningful ways. This video project assessment requires a minimum of 40 instructional minutes over at least two and a half class periods. This particular example is appropriate for fourth through sixth graders.

Lesson 1: Static and Dynamic Balance Concepts

This lesson reviews these concepts and allows students to explore and practice applications.

Starting the Lesson

- Review the concepts of static balance (balance used when holding a pose or remaining motionless) and dynamic balance (balance used when in motion or traveling, or starting and stopping).
- Review how each of these concepts can be found in various physical activities (sports, recreation, dance, martial arts) and how they can be used together to form complex movement patterns.

Developing the Lesson

- Have students select several physical activities with which they are familiar as well as activities they would like to know more about.

Examples of Uses of Static and Dynamic Balance

Bowling
Static balance—the setup (preparatory phase of the approach and delivery)
Dynamic balance—approach and delivery of the ball
Football
Static balance—three-point stance
Dynamic balance—moving from the on-line position to a running position
Track and field, running events
Static balance—set position in the blocks
Dynamic balance—leaving the blocks

- Then have students find examples of movement patterns that require the use of static and dynamic balance for each of the selected physical activities.
- Review concepts for balancing on an object (take your time, look at the end of the object, and so on).
- Direct students to practice combinations of static and dynamic balances for various physical activities on a balance beam.

Closing the Lesson

- Introduce the concept of designing a movement sequence linking movements together (highlighting static and dynamic balance) that may include examples from the class activity.
- Students may find other examples of static and dynamic balances used in physical activities. This could be used as a homework assignment for the next class.

Lesson 2: Static and Dynamic Balance Movement Sequence

This lesson reviews these concepts and helps students focus on learning movement sequences using these concepts.

Starting the Lesson

- Review the concepts of static and dynamic balance and movement sequence development. Reinforce the importance of smooth transitions between static and dynamic balance skills.

Developing the Lesson

- Distribute and explain the worksheet for designing a movement sequence. This worksheet requires the student to identify static and dynamic balance positions for three different physical activities and develop a movement sequence by linking the balances for the three activities.
- For static balances, allow students to either name (i.e., stork stand, 3 point stance) or draw the pose. For dynamic balances, require students to name each (run to base, step approach in bowling).
- Give students time to practice the movement sequence using the performance cues highlighted on the worksheet.

Closing the Lesson

- Discuss the importance of practice to a skillful performance. Explain that to demonstrate proficiency in the movement sequence, the students will need to practice outside of the physical education class period.
- Discuss strategies for practicing outside of class; for example, draw a line on the playground to practice at recess or visualize it on the bus ride to school.
- Give each student a photocopy of his or her completed worksheet to use to practice the movement sequence. You may also wish to set up a homework practice calendar.

Lesson 3: Video Day

The big day! The chance for students to show what they've learned and practiced. Organize a videotaping station and make sure the rest of the students are practicing their sequences so no time is wasted. For safety's sake be sure you're able to provide adequate supervision to all students. Remember, the videotaping allows you to evaluate outside of class time.

Starting the Lesson

- Introduce videotaping protocols:
  1. Order of student performance—Establish a means for identifying which students are performing the movement sequence and when, practicing the movement sequence, and participating in the class activity. In my classes, students perform in the order of the learning team: The first person on the blue team performs first while the next person in the line waits "on-deck," and so on.

Chapter 3 introduced the concept of learning teams as a management strategy. Assign the students to learning teams at the beginning of the school year based on teacher-selected criteria (e.g., skills, gender, learning needs, and leadership qualities) for establishing a balanced grouping of students. This strategy is especially useful during psychomotor testing if you assign a performance order within each team. This will help you efficiently record student assessment data on a master sheet.

While one learning team is engaged in the videotaping process, the other three teams are involved in a class activity. I have found it best to have students engaged in a skill I have already taught but that students may still need to practice. That way, they can work more independently while I focus on the learning team I am assessing by allowing me to monitor the progress of the learning team being assessed.

  2. On-camera information—The student should stand in front of the camera, say his or her first and last name, and then hold up the completed worksheet. Then have the child perform his or her routine.
  3. On-deck behavior—Students in the learning team waiting to perform for the camera are "on-deck." Provide equipment nearby but out of view of the video camera and encourage on-deck students to rehearse their routines while they are waiting for their turns. Other team members can peer assess the routines, which helps improve the accuracy of the routines and provides an opportunity to practice.

Developing the Lesson

- Having someone else film the students leaves you free to manage and supervise the rest of the students. The video camera can be operated by any of the following: classroom student teacher, parent volunteer, paraprofessional (teacher's aide), or high school audiovisual club student. Make sure the camera operators are familiar with the filming protocols and how to operate a video camera. On the other hand, you may find that operating the camera yourself while allowing a classroom teacher or paraprofessional to supervise the class activities reduces the time you need to spend later reviewing the videotape.

- Be sure to keep an eye on the rest of the class as they practice a familiar activity. If you're lucky enough to have an aide or trained volunteer for this purpose, remember you are still ultimately responsible for student safety. This is where videotaping can be a real management boon.

Closing the Lesson

- Provide students with an opportunity to comment and share concerns regarding the video project. Take notes during this session. Children have great ideas that you may wish to incorporate into an upcoming video project.

Chapter 8

Reporting to Parents

Cumulative portfolios travel with the student throughout his or her school career and may be used as a method for reporting the student's progress. A cumulative portfolio offers a snapshot of the student's development from year to year in several subject areas, including physical education entries. A physical education cumulative portfolio entry should provide information related to the student's demonstrated ability to perform motor skills, understand movement concepts and skills, and use appropriate self- and social responsibility skills. It should also provide the student with an opportunity to self-assess his or her development in these areas.

Year End Summary Sheet: A Cumulative Portfolio Entry Method

One strategy that addresses each of these issues is the year-end summary (YES). To use YES, at the close of the school year, have each student complete a double-sided summary sheet. Like the sample provided in this chapter, design this sheet as a self-assessment tool that will help both you and the student determine if the student can perform and comprehend the skills, knowledge, and behaviors you have emphasized in physical education the past school year. Be sure the assessment items you choose represent the psychomotor, cognitive, and affective domains and reflect the physical education curriculum at each grade level. This, however, should not include other information regarding actual performance ratings by the physical educator (e.g., rubrics of skill performance, and so on). These belong in the 1-5 Physical Education Portfolio.

In the sample, the first side of the summary sheet requires the student to reflect on his or

Self-Assessment Symbols

Design symbols such as the following to help a student respond quickly yet accurately.

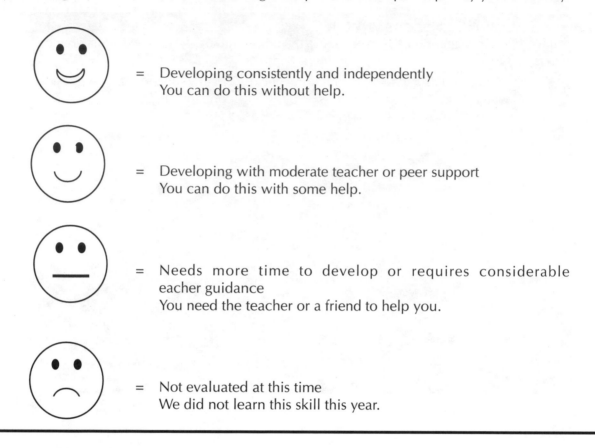

= Developing consistently and independently
You can do this without help.

= Developing with moderate teacher or peer support
You can do this with some help.

= Needs more time to develop or requires considerable eacher guidance
You need the teacher or a friend to help you.

= Not evaluated at this time
We did not learn this skill this year.

her ability to use various movement skills. This is the "reflecting side." The sidebar above shows symbols the student could use to streamline the self-assessment process.

The second side of the sample summary sheet is the "doing side." It requires the student to demonstrate his or her understanding of the skills, concepts, and behaviors necessary for successful participation in physical education.

Adjust YES sheets so they are age appropriate. For example, have first grade students select an appropriate answer from a choice bank provided on the YES sheet. Ask questions on the second grade YES sheet that can be answered with one word. Require short answers of students in grades three, four, and five. You may need to read items aloud so nonreaders can understand and follow along while completing the YES sheet.

Report Cards

A cumulative portfolio is not the only method educators are using for reporting student learning. Your school district may use a more traditional method, such as a report card. Although convenient to use, reports card may not provide sufficient information about the development of a student. By using one of the following suggestions, you can enhance the information reported to parents on a report card:

- Use the YES sheet as a teacher evaluation checklist. In this situation, as the physical educator, you rate the student on each skill and concept, using assessment data you've collected during the school year. Then include this sheet with the report card.

- Use key phrases to communicate the meaning of a numeric grade, letter grade, or other symbolic system (e.g., S = Satisfactory). The key phrase concept also works well alone or in combination with any of the other reporting systems (numbers, letters, or symbols). Work out a system that helps you streamline your workload; for example, the following key phrases could be relied upon:

  100%-85% O = Outstanding (Key phrase: Developing consistently and independently)

  84%-69% S = Satisfactory (Key phrase: Developing with moderate teacher or peer support)

  68%-0% NI = Needs Improvement (Key phrase: Requires considerable teacher guidance and needs more time to develop)

I use a YES sheet for first through fifth grades based on the skills, knowledge, and behaviors important in my elementary physical education program. Feel free to customize the sheets to reflect the important parts of your program. Parents may also want to know on the YES sheet how the information relates to grades. For example, they might be concerned that a child has been penalized for responding honestly to self-assessment questions. A cover letter explaining your approach may eliminate confusion.

PHYSICAL EDUCATION SUMMARY WORKSHEET

NAME _____ DATE _____

FOR SCHOOL YEAR _____ TO _____ 1st GRADE: PART 1

Listed below are skills we learn about in first grade. I have asked your child to rate his or her perceived ability to use each of the skills.

Additional information related to your child's progress in physical education is available in the 1-5 Physical Education Portfolio. If you would like to review your child's portfolio, please contact Ms. Schiemer.

Draw a mouth on the face to show how well you can do each activity.

I can . . .

🙂 Jump

🙂 Hop

🙂 Gallop

🙂 Slide

🙂 Bounce a ball with one hand

🙂 Animal Walk (Moving from hands to feet)

🙂 Balance on body parts

🙂 Forward curled roll

🙂 Dodge (Change direction quickly)

🙂 Work well with others

Most classes I choose behaviors that are . . .

PHYSICAL EDUCATION SUMMARY WORKSHEET

NAME _____ DATE _____

FOR SCHOOL YEAR ____ TO ____ 1st GRADE: PART 2

1. Circle the movement that has a two-footed takeoff and two-footed landing:

2. Circle the movements that use only one foot for takeoff and landing:

3. Circle the movement that uses one foot as the leader foot and the other foot as the follower:

4. Circle the movement that can go only to the left side or the right side:

5. When you bounce a ball with one hand what should you do?

6. When you are balancing what should you do?

PHYSICAL EDUCATION SUMMARY WORKSHEET

7. When you are rolling forward what should you do?

8. When you are faking another person what should you do?

PHYSICAL EDUCATION SUMMARY WORKSHEET

NAME _____ DATE _____

FOR SCHOOL YEAR ____ TO ____ 2nd GRADE: PART 1

Listed below are skills we learn about in second grade. I have asked your child to rate his or her perceived ability to use each of the skills.

Additional information related to your child's progress in physical education is available in the 1-5 Physical Education Portfolio. If you would like to review your child's portfolio, please contact Ms. Schiemer.

I can . . .

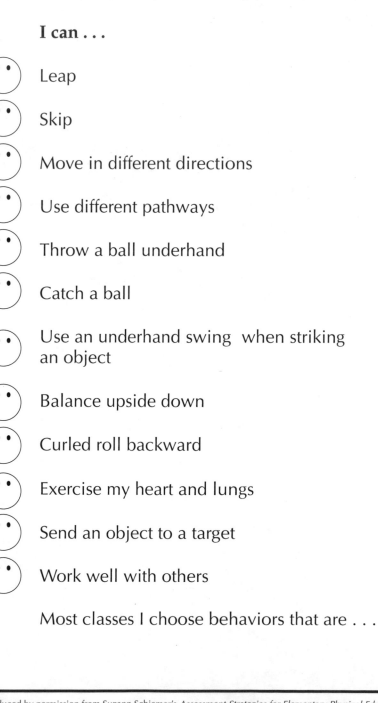

Leap

Skip

Move in different directions

Use different pathways

Throw a ball underhand

Catch a ball

Use an underhand swing when striking
an object

Balance upside down

Curled roll backward

Exercise my heart and lungs

Send an object to a target

Work well with others

Most classes I choose behaviors that are . . .

PHYSICAL EDUCATION SUMMARY WORKSHEET

NAME _____ DATE _____

FOR SCHOOL YEAR _____ TO _____ 2nd GRADE: PART 2

1. What is it called when you take off on one foot and land on the other foot?

2. What is it called when you step and hop on one foot and then step and hop on the other foot?

3. List four different directions the body can move: _____, _____, _____, _____

4. Draw and name the three different pathways. _____, _____, _____

5. List two important things about throwing a ball underhand correctly. _____, _____

6. List two important things about catching a ball correctly. _____, _____

7. What will I see when you balance upside down?

8. List two important things about rolling backward with good form. _____, _____

9. How can you get your heart to beat faster?

10. List two important things you should do when throwing at a target to help you hit it. _____, _____

PHYSICAL EDUCATION SUMMARY WORKSHEET

NAME _____ DATE _____

FOR SCHOOL YEAR _____ TO _____ 3rd GRADE: PART 1

Listed below are skills we learn about in third grade. I have asked your child to rate his or her perceived ability to use each of the skills.

Additional information related to your child's progress in physical education is available in the 1-5 Physical Education Portfolio. If you would like to review your child's portfolio, please contact Ms. Schiemer.

I can . . .

- Use force to move an object

- Throw an object from the side of my body

- Catch an object thrown from the side of the body

- Use a sidearm swing to strike an object

- Dribble an object with my hands

- Balance with a partner (countertension & counterbalance)

- Stretch the muscles of my body safely

- Move (reposition) to gain control of an object

- Work well with others

Most classes I choose behaviors that are . . .

PHYSICAL EDUCATION SUMMARY WORKSHEET

NAME _____ DATE _____

FOR SCHOOL YEAR ____ TO ____ 3rd GRADE: PART 2

1. List two important things you learned about using force effectively:

2. List three important things you know about throwing an object from the side of the body so it goes where you want it to.

3. List three important things you know about striking an object from the side of the body so it goes where you want it to.

4. List two important things you do when dribbling an object with your hands.

5. What is a counterbalance (draw or explain with words)?

6. What can you do if you are flexible?

7. List two things you should do to gain control of an object.

PHYSICAL EDUCATION SUMMARY WORKSHEET

NAME _____ DATE _____

FOR SCHOOL YEAR _____ TO _____ 4th GRADE: PART 1

Listed below are skills we learn about in fourth grade. I have asked your child to rate his or her perceived ability to use each of the skills.

Additional information related to your child's progress in physical education is available in the 1-5 Physical Education Portfolio. If you would like to review your child's portfolio, please contact Ms. Schiemer.

I can . . .

☺ Throw an object overhand

☺ Catch an object thrown overhand by a partner

☺ Use an overhand swing to strike an object

☺ Dribble an object with my feet

☺ Kick an object far

☺ Use the skills of takeoff and landing when going over or onto an object

☺ Exercise my muscles to build strength and endurance for activities

☺ Keep control of an object against an opponent (open space)

☺ Work well with others

Most classes I choose behaviors that are . . .

PHYSICAL EDUCATION SUMMARY WORKSHEET

NAME _____ DATE _____

FOR SCHOOL YEAR _____ TO _____ 4th GRADE: PART 2

1. List three important things you know about throwing an object overhand effectively.

2. List three important things you know about catching an object.

3. List three important things you know about dribbling an object with your feet.

4. List three important things to do when kicking an object for distance.

5. Name one physical activity that uses a takeoff and landing.

6. Name one skill or exercise that uses muscular endurance.

7. List two things you should do to keep control of an object.

PHYSICAL EDUCATION SUMMARY WORKSHEET

NAME _____ DATE _____

FOR SCHOOL YEAR ____ TO ____ 5th GRADE: PART 1

Listed below are skills we learn about in fifth grade. I have asked your child to rate his or her perceived ability to use each of the skills.
Additional information related to your child's progress in physical education is available in the 1-5 Physical Education Portfolio. If you would like to review your child's portfolio, please contact Ms. Schiemer.

I can . . .

Punt an object far

Volley an object with my hands

Volley with a racket

Dribble an object with an implement

Self-assess my aerobic endurance

Self-assess my flexibility

Self-assess my muscular strength and endurance

Ability to apply game tactics (offense and defense)

Use guarding strategies

Work well with others

Most classes I choose behaviors that are . . .

PHYSICAL EDUCATION SUMMARY WORKSHEET

NAME _____ DATE _____

FOR SCHOOL YEAR ____ TO ____ 5th: PART 2

1. How is punting an object different from kicking an object?

2. List three important things you know about volleying an object effectively.

3. List two physical activities that use the skill of volleying.

4. List three important things you know about dribbling an object with an implement.

5. List two physical activities that use the skill of dribbling with an implement.

6. Name one health-related fitness self-assessment for each:
   Aerobic endurance—
   Flexibility—
   Muscular strength and endurance—

7. Define these two words:
   Offense—
   Defense—

References

Bredekamp, S., and T. Rosegrant, eds. 1992. *Reaching Potentials: Appropriate Curriculum and Assessment for Young Children.* Washington, DC: National Association for the Education of Young Children.

Franck, M., G. Graham, H. Lawson, T. Loughrey, R. Ritson, M. Sanborn, and V. Seefeldt. 1991. *Physical Education Outcomes: A Project of the National Association for Sport & Physical Education.* Reston, VA: NASPE.

Graham, G. 1992. *Teaching Children Physical Education: Becoming a Master Teacher.* Champaign, IL: Human Kinetics.

Grady, E. 1992. *The Portfolio Approach to Assessment.* Bloomington, IN: Phi Delta Kappa Educational Foundation.

Hebert, E.A. 1992. "Portfolios Invite Reflection—From Students and Staff." *Educational Leadership* 49(8): 58-61.

———., and L. Schultz. 1996. "The Power of Portfolios." *Educational Leadership* 53(7): 70-71.

Hellison, D.R. 1985. *Goals and Strategies for Teaching Physical Education.* Champaign, IL: Human Kinetics.

Hellison, D.R., and T.J. Templin. 1991. *A Reflective Approach to Teaching Physical Education.* Champaign, IL: Human Kinetics.

Kelly, L.E. 1988. "Curriculum Design Model." *Journal of Physical Education, Recreation and Dance* 59(6): 26-32.

———. 1989. "Instructional Time: The Overlooked Factor in PE Curriculum Development." *Journal of Physical Education, Recreation and Dance* 60(6): 29-32.

Khattri, N., M.B. Kane, and A.L. Reeve. 1995. "How Performance Assessments Affect Teaching and Learning." *Educational Leadership* 53(3): 80-83.

Melograno, V.J. 1998. *Professional and Student Portfolios for Physical Education.* Champaign, IL: Human Kinetics.

National Association for Sport & Physical Education (NASPE). 1995. *Moving Into the Future: National Physical Education Standards.* St. Louis: Mosby.

Perrone, V., ed. 1991. *Expanding Student Assessment.* Alexandria, VA: Association for Supervision and Curriculum Development.

Shepard, L.A. 1995. "Using Assessment to Improve Learning." *Educational Leadership* 52(5): 38-43.

Thomas, J.R., A.M. Lee, and K.T. Thomas. 1988. *Physical Education for Children: Concepts Into Practice.* Champaign, IL: Human Kinetics.

Wiggins, G. 1992. "Creating Tests Worth Taking." *Educational Leadership* 50(8): 26-33.

About the Author

Suzann Schiemer, a K-5 physical education specialist in Bloomsburg, Pennsylvania, is a nationally recognized expert in assessing student learning.

Physical education programs that Suzann helped institute at two elementary schools received Outstanding Program Awards from the Pennsylvania State Association for Health, Physical Education, Recreation and Dance.

Suzann was the keynote speaker on the topic of assessment at the 1994 and 1995 National Conferences on Teaching Children's Physical Education and the 1997 Conference for the Council for Children's Expanded Physical Education. All three keynote presentations were by invitation at highly respected conferences known for promoting quality physical education programs for children.

Suzann was selected for inclusion in the 1998 edition of *Who's Who Among America's Teachers*. High school students cited for academic excellence are invited to nominate one teacher from their academic experience for inclusion in the publication.

Suzann is an assessment consultant for numerous in-services and workshops throughout the United States. She is a contributing author to the articles *Physical Education— Learning is for Everyone* (PE-Life) and *Designing Assessments: Applications for Physical Education*. She is a member of the American Alliance of Health, Physical Education, Recreation and Dance and the Association for Supervision and Curriculum Development.